The Twelve Steps—

A Spiritual Journey

The Twelve Steps—
A SPIRITUAL JOURNEY

*A Working Guide for Adult Children
from Addictive and Other Dysfunctional Families*

Based on Biblical Teachings

Friends in Recovery

Recovery Publications
1201 Knoxville Street
San Diego, CA 92110
(619) 275-1350

Published by
Recovery Publications
1201 Knoxville Street
San Diego, CA 92110
(619) 275-1350

All the scripture quotations are from the New International Version of the Bible.

The Twelve Steps have been reprinted and adapted with permission from Alcoholics Anonymous World Services, Inc. For purposes of this workbook, the word "alcoholic" in Step One has been changed to read "the effects of our separation from God," and the word "alcoholics" in Step Twelve has been changed to read "others."

The Twelve Steps—A Spiritual Journey represents the experiences and opinions of Friends in Recovery. Opinions expressed herein are not to be attributed to Alcoholics Anonymous as a whole, nor does *The Twelve Steps—A Spiritual Journey* imply any endorsement by Alcoholics Anonymous.

Printed in the United States of America
Second Printing March 1989
Third Printing November 1989

Recovery Publications

The Twelve Steps—A Spiritual Journey: A Working Guide for Adult Children from Addictive and Other Dysfunctional Families. Based on Biblical Teachings.

1.   2.   1. Title
ISBN: 0941405-02-8 pbk $14.95

*In memory of Richard, Edward and the countless others
whose lives were a struggle with addiction, and
who never discovered a spiritual path to recovery.*

*This book is especially dedicated to those family members
and friends who have found the courage to seek recovery.*

*In appreciation of the many individuals who participated in
researching and preparing the materials used in this text.
Their willingness to participate and provide feedback was a
vital contribution to this book.*

TABLE OF CONTENTS

THE TWELVE STEPS OF ALCOHOLICS ANONYMOUS

1. We admitted we were powerless over alcohol—that our lives had become unmanageable.

2. Came to believe that a Power greater than ourselves could restore us to sanity.

3. Made a decision to turn our will and our lives over to the care of God as we understood Him.

4. Made a searching and fearless moral inventory of ourselves.

5. Admitted to God, to ourselves, and to another human being the exact nature of our wrongs.

6. Were entirely ready to have God remove all these defects of character.

7. Humbly asked Him to remove our shortcomings.

8. Made a list of all persons we had harmed, and became willing to make amends to them all.

9. Made direct amends to such people wherever possible, except when to do so would injure them or others.

10. Continued to take personal inventory and when we were wrong promptly admitted it.

11. Sought through prayer and meditation to improve our conscious contact with God as we understood Him, praying only for knowledge of His will for us and the power to carry that out.

12. Having had a spiritual awakening as the result of these steps, we tried to carry this message to alcoholics, and to practice these principles in all our affairs.

Reprinted with permission of **Alcoholics Anonymous, World Services, Inc.**

THE TWELVE STEPS AND
YOUR SPIRITUAL PILGRIMAGE

The Twelve Steps is not a program sponsored by any particular religious group or entity. Though people using this program find it harmonious with their own personal theology and spiritual beliefs, it has no official religious affiliation. It is, however, a program that helps us to rediscover and deepen the spiritual part of ourselves and recognize its importance in our lives. We learn to live our lives according to the guidance of our Higher Power, God. We realize that the void or despair we have felt is caused by ignoring or rejecting our relationship with our Lord, Jesus Christ.

With God's power, The Twelve Step Program becomes an empowering tool to relieve our suffering, fill our emptiness, and help us extend God's presence in our lives. This will release great quantities of energy, love, and joy, which we have never before known. It is a program that we follow at our own pace, in our own way, with God's help and the support of others who are in the Program. All we need is an open mind and a willingness to try. Much of the work will be done by God working through us. We will suddenly notice improvements in ourselves: our awareness, our sensitivity, our ability to love, to be free. We will often be surprised by our own spiritual and emotional growth.

The purpose of this workbook is to illustrate the Twelve Steps as a recovery tool, fully integrated as an ongoing part of our spiritual pilgrimage. The book uses Biblical insight to help us identify and deal with issues that are interfering with our lives. As we work through the problems, relying on the dynamics of the Twelve Steps, we will experience recovery that initiates physical, emotional, and spiritual well-being.

Trust in God's guidance is necessary when completing the work. In this Program, it is important to realize that it is God's desire that we be returned to wholeness. He will give us the courage to work and struggle in order to succeed. Keeping a positive attitude will be very helpful in our recovery process. Negative thoughts can be damaging and will slow our progress. As we surrender to the process of working each Step, we realize we are in God's presence and our negative feelings are minimized. There is no right or wrong way to work the material. Timing will vary among individuals; however, each person will experience growth and change.

The material in this book focuses on the individual, and is being used successfully in groups as a Step Study Writing Workshop. The format used in these workshops includes forming small "family groups" with a limit of six people per family. These "family groups" work together for a portion of the meeting, and then gather as one group during the final segment for general sharing.

These workshops will be the source of many benefits and rewards. The experience of being in a small family group creates an atmosphere wherein healthy family-type communications can develop. It is a safe environment where trust can be learned. As individuals share their early experiences of growing up in emotionally repressive or troubled homes, they come to recognize the damage that has been done and their need for healing. The small "family groups" provide an arena for quality sharing, wherein family secrets no longer need to be hidden, and the process of loving self-parenting can begin.

Workshop participation is an important step in breaking out of the isolation often experienced by Adult Children. An important part of this process is feeling safe in the "family group." Using the Steps as the central tool, along with the support of the "family group," it becomes possible to express long suppressed shame, anger and grief. Individuals are encouraged to release and let go of the past, thus making room for the lightness, serenity and calmness which comes as a result of working the Steps.

As the title implies, the Twelve Steps are a spiritual journey which can be used as a way out of self destructive behavior, as well as a laboratory in which to learn new behavior. It provides an opportunity to experience feelings, talk openly with others, enjoy life one day at a time, and develop healthy relationships. Working together in a group can be a powerful and transforming process. Loneliness will lessen as friendships among group members develop. Individuals can learn to be close to others, by giving as well as receiving comfort and support. Communication outside of the meeting is a vital element in the workshop process. Participants are encouraged to use the telephone and other ways to socialize outside of the regular meeting time.

The Twelve Step material used in this book is meant to be a framework upon which our own life experiences can be reviewed with love and courage. We realize we have reached this point knowing very little about ourselves. As we develop a deeper relationship with God, more will be disclosed to us. Slowly we will be given the strength to put the past behind us and build a new life. The depth of our relationship with God will be increased as our lives becomes less and less compromised. Successful completion of this workbook and a commitment to work the Steps as a daily routine for the rest of our lives will provide us with the ongoing gift of peace and serenity.

Give freely of yourself and join us. We shall be with you in the Fellowship of God's Holy Spirit.

GOD BLESS YOU.

INTRODUCTION

The Twelve Steps—A Spiritual Journey is a comprehensive working guide that enables the user to gain an understanding of the spiritual power of the Twelve Steps when worked within a Christian perspective. This material is intended to reach those individuals who experienced trauma or some type of deprivation in childhood. The focus of this material is directed primarily to adults whose childhoods where traumatically affected by chemically dependent, violent or other dysfunctional behaviors from the responsible adults. Since the founding of Alcoholics Anonymous in 1935, the Twelve Steps have become a way for many millions of people to change the course of their lives.

This book contains scriptural passages that illustrate the compatibility between the practice of Christianity and the working of the Twelve Steps. The material is not based on a creed or specific statements of faith from any particular denomination. Its goal is to provide an understanding of the Twelve Steps within a Biblical context. When used as intended, the Steps are profoundly powerful tools for allowing God to heal damaged emotions. This book constitutes a spiritual program that helps us regain balance and order, and leads us to full restoration of health and happiness through a renewed relationship with God.

The fact that God's plan for us is revealed in the Holy Scriptures is easily accepted by those of us who are Christians. Both mature Christians and those who are just being awakened to a personal relationship with God can find tremendous value in the Twelve Steps. By applying them to the events of one's life on a daily basis, they become an effective means for enriching one's relationship with God and allowing His plan for us to unfold. The Steps are especially powerful when used in conjunction with the regular Christian practices of prayer and Bible study. We will discover the unique ways in which the Holy Scriptures support and expand our understanding of the Steps.

The twelve-step process of recovery is a spiritual journey. It takes us from a life where we experience confusion and grief to one of peace and serenity. Many changes can and will come over us, but they won't necessarily happen all at once. The process takes time, and patience. God will in His time instill in us the strength of character that only comes from a healthy relationship with Him.

Commitment to recovery will be strengthened by our growing trust in ourselves and others. An important sign of recovery occurs when we become more open and communicative, and begin to value the counsel of others who are sharing this program of recovery. People who are participating in this program with us will become an important part of our lives. We will learn what open sharing can do for us when we become willing to reveal ourselves to others.

We may have many self-defeating habits or behaviors that need correcting. When looking at our methods of relating, it is important to remember the way in which these patterns began. Because of the chaotic conditions in which we were raised, we developed behaviors that now sabotage and assault the successful management of our lives as adults. Having grown up in emotionally repressive families, we became accustomed to denying our pain and discomfort. During our early years, most of us found it necessary to shut down our feelings and "keep everything locked inside." We learned in childhood that expressing our own wants and needs caused rejection. This rejection stimulated the growth of intense feelings of inadequacy. It seemed to us that, no matter how hard we tried, things always got worse.

As adults, we sometimes find it difficult to accept the reality of our pasts. This has kept us from seeing the disabling behaviors we have developed. In our present environments, we may experience pain, fear and rage that cannot be expressed freely. Repressing our true feelings is a result of our continuing to view our environment as we did in childhood. When we express our needs openly, we risk being rejected. Rather than risking rejection, many of us compensate for our repressed feelings by doing things to extremes. Our behavior may range from being overly involved in work, over-eating or using mood-altering substances such as drugs and alcohol.

For many of us, denial has been a major tool for survival. Denial is a learned pattern of behavior and, as such, is incredibly cunning. We can consciously deny reality by telling a blatant lie to hide some truth about ourself or someone else. Conversely, we can be unaware of our denial by the secrets we keep from ourselves. Denial can block any and all reality from our minds. It cleverly protects us from realizing the consequences of our actions, because we simply do not acknowledge any responsibility for them. The power of denial is represented Biblically by Peter in his denial of Christ. It was less painful for Peter to deny that he was a follower of Christ than to face the consequences of admitting his relationship with Him. Peter's fear of recrimination and rebuke was stronger than his love for Jesus. In a similar way, we prefer to continue behavior that "saves face," rather than to acknowledge reality and accept the consequences of our actions. We find it easier to hide from our true feelings by being seemingly over-attentive to our families, our churches and our jobs. Staying busy allows us to ignore our true feelings, thereby denying them.

As we enter this program of recovery and begin to look honestly at ourselves, we see the damage that has resulted from our personal history of dysfunction. God has given us free will, which makes it possible for us to choose alternative ways of relating to the events in our lives and to those around us. It is important to set aside some of our childhood messages and begin the work of learning new behaviors that will better serve our highest good. Rather than filling our lives to overflowing with activities, we need time to be with our Lord in prayer and quietness. Through prayer and the competent exercise of our free will, we will learn to make healthier choices.

Our lives to this point are comprised of all of our experiences. We do not always know the extent of the damage that has been done to us or to others in our lives. The pain of remembering is simply too great. No matter how hard we try to forget their presence, these memories continue to be driving forces in our lives. Inappropriate behavior continues to surface, and we must learn that, in order to change it, we must accept the past and deal with it honestly.

Some of us have been taught to believe that, if we are Christians, our lives will "automatically" be in order, and we will experience peace and serenity. As reassuring as this may seem, it is rarely possible to find someone raised in a dysfunctional situation who does not experience some form of disabling behavior. For some, intense devotion to religion makes them feel guilty, because they know their lives are in turmoil.

For Christians who suffer from an addictive disease, or who are the product of a family with addictive traits, the Church's judgmental messages can be especially troublesome. They can keep a person from seeking recovery. To admit to imperfection might mean that we are not good Christians. However, as true recovery begins and the Twelve Steps are worked, we see that all of us need help, comfort and courage to face our problems.

As we become willing to admit our dysfunction to ourselves and others in recovery, we will see that this process is healing and rewarding. Our Christian walk will be enhanced by the fact that we stop the denial and become honest with ourselves and others. This alone will start an important phase of healing.

As we begin to acknowledge and even befriend our negative or repressed nature, we see, even as we stand in the sunlight, that we cast a "shadow." Standing before the Lord and seeking His guidance does not automatically relieve us of the burdens cast by our "shadow." However, we will find that by facing it squarely, with God's help, the darkness slowly diminishes as our strength and health return.

By diligently working the material in this book, we will be able to reexamine our relationship with God and discover new ways in which He can empower our daily lives. We will learn to look fearlessly at our "shadow," and to accept our unwanted tendencies such as anger, inappropriate sexual behavior, hostility or aggression. Remember, this process includes inviting Jesus to help us redefine the limits we set for ourselves as we discover that "all things are possible for those who love the Lord."

This Twelve Step Program enables us to reclaim our birthright as children of God. We are created in God's image and have unlimited gifts available to us. The journey we are about to begin will awaken us to God's creation and give us an opportunity to experience peaceful and productive living. He will help us heal our damaged emotions. Feelings of unworthiness, anxiety and inferiority will disappear. Focusing on our new relationship with God will eliminate our obsessive need for other people's approval. Our attention will be captivated by the promise of the wonderful adventure calling us to a new life in Jesus Christ.

GOD BLESS YOU

THE TWELVE STEPS AND RELATED SCRIPTURE

STEP ONE

We admitted we were powerless over our separation from God—that our lives had become unmanageable.

I know nothing good lives in me, that is, in my sinful nature. For I have the desire to do what is good, but I cannot carry it out. (Romans 7:18)

STEP TWO

Came to believe that a power greater than ourselves could restore us to sanity.

For it is God who works in you to will and to act according to his good purpose. (Philippians 2:13)

STEP THREE

Made a decision to turn our will and our lives over to the care of God as we understood Him.

Therefore, I urge you, brothers, in view of God's mercy, to offer your bodies as living sacrifices, holy and pleasing to God—which is your spiritual worship. (Romans 12:1)

STEP FOUR

Made a searching and fearless moral inventory of ourselves.

Let us examine our ways and test them, and let us return to the Lord. (Lamentations 3:40)

STEP FIVE

Admitted to God, to ourselves, and to another human being the exact nature of our wrongs.

> *Therefore confess your sins to each other and pray for each other so that you may be healed. (James 5:16a)*

STEP SIX

Were entirely ready to have God remove all these defects of character.

> *Humble yourselves before the Lord, and he will lift you up. (James 4:10)*

STEP SEVEN

Humbly asked Him to remove our shortcomings.

> *If we confess our sins, he is faithful and just and will forgive us our sins and purify us from all unrighteousness. (1 John 1:9)*

STEP EIGHT

Made a list of all persons we had harmed and became willing to make amends to them all.

> *Do to others as you would have them do to you. (Luke 6:31)*

STEP NINE

Made direct amends to such people wherever possible, except when to do so would injure them or others.

> *Therefore, if you are offering your gift at the altar and there remember that your brother has something against you, leave your gift there in front of the altar. First go and be reconciled to your brother; then come and offer your gift. (Matthew 5:23-24)*

STEP TEN

Continued to take personal inventory and, when we were wrong, promptly admitted it.

> *So, if you think you are standing firm, be careful that you don't fall. (1 Corinthians 10:12)*

STEP ELEVEN

Sought through prayer and meditation to improve our conscious contact with God as we understood Him, praying only for knowledge of His will for us and the power to carry that out.

> *Let the word of Christ dwell in you richly. (Colossians 3:16a)*

STEP TWELVE

Having had a spiritual awakening as the result of these steps, we tried to carry this message to others, and to practice these principles in all our affairs.

> *Brothers, if someone is caught in a sin, you who are spiritual should restore him gently. But watch yourself, or you also may be tempted. (Galatians 6:1)*

PREPARATORY INFORMATION
FOR STEP STUDY GROUPS

APPENDIX ONE contains suggested methods of study for people participating in a Step Study Writing Workshop. The recommendations are based on the personal experiences of many people who have used the materials. This section provides specific guidelines for starting and conducting a Step Study Writing Workshop.

APPENDIX TWO includes sample meeting designs and useful suggestions for conducting a Step Study Writing Workshop.

APPENDIX THREE contains weekly exercises to be used during each meeting. These exercises are valuable tools for groups discussing the materials relative to the Step being studied.

NOTICE

This book is designed to provide information regarding the subject matter covered. It is provided with the understanding that the publisher and author are not engaged in rendering individualized professional services. These processes and questions are intended for group or individual study, and not designed to be a substitute for one-to-one professional therapy when such help is necessary.

NOTE FROM THE PUBLISHER

Those who participated in the writing and review of this material are recovering Christian lay people and clergy. Their intention is to carry the message of the Twelve Steps and Christ's love to all hurting people. Central to the theme of this work is that healing is possible for those individuals whose childhood has been impacted by addictive or emotionally repressive parents or responsible adults. The talent and insight they brought to this book were founded in the belief that, through Scripture and the Twelve Steps, God's love and wisdom could restore hurting Christians to wholeness.

Their intention is to offer a workable tool for writing one's own personal story of recovery. This has been achieved by incorporating the proven wisdom of Bible truths and the Twelve Steps as adapted from Alcoholics Anonymous. The material emphasizes self-understanding and the unchanging love of God for all humanity.

The philosophical foundation for this book is based on the Twelve Step concept that has helped hundreds of thousands of individuals recover from many forms of addictive, compulsive or obsessive behavior. The Twelve Traditions of Alcoholics Anonymous stress personal anonymity as a vital element in personal recovery. "Friends in Recovery" have chosen to remain anonymous to pursue their personal recovery.

As "Friends in Recovery," we place our confidence in the person of Jesus Christ, rather than in principles. We offer these materials, not as an end in themselves, but as a means to developing a healthy relationship with God and with others.

COMMON BEHAVIOR CHARACTERISTICS
OF ADULT CHILDREN

Research involving chemically dependent or emotionally repressed individuals and their families has determined that certain behavior characteristics are common in adult children from these homes. The behaviors reveal an underlying structure of disorder which is damaging to those involved. Although the general population demonstrates many of the behaviors, individuals from dysfunctional families tend to have a higher incidence of these characteristics. This exercise is intended to help you identify whether or not these are areas of your life in which dysfunctional behavior characteristics are evident.

We have feelings of low self-esteem that cause us to judge ourselves and others without mercy. We try to cover up or compensate by being perfectionistic, caretaking, controlling, contemptuous and gossipy.

- In what ways do you think, feel or act in an effort to compensate for your feelings of low self-esteem? _____

_____

_____

_____

We tend to isolate ourselves and to feel uneasy around other people, especially authority figures.

- Give examples of how you isolate yourself from other people. _____

_____

_____

_____

- What difficulty do you have dealing with people in authority? _____

_____

_____

_____

We are approval seekers and will do anything to make people like us. We are extremely loyal even in the face of evidence that indicates loyalty is undeserved.

- In what ways do you seek approval from your family or friends? _____

_____

_____

- Cite an example where your extreme loyalty is undeserved. _____

_____

_____

_____

1

We are intimidated by angry people and personal criticism. This causes us to feel anxious and overly sensitive.

- What is your first recollection of being intimidated by an angry person? _____
  _____
  _____
  _____

- How do you respond to personal criticism? _____
  _____
  _____
  _____

We habitually choose to have relationships with emotionally unavailable people with addictive personalities. We are usually less attracted to healthy, caring people.

- Describe your relationships involving people with addictive/compulsive personality styles
  (e.g. alcoholic, workaholic, gambler, overeater, religious fanatic). _____
  _____
  _____
  _____

- Describe the relationships from which you receive nurture and support. _____
  _____
  _____
  _____

We live life as victims and are attracted to other victims in our love and friendship relationships. We confuse love with pity and tend to "love" people we can pity and rescue.

- Describe an instance in which you were drawn into a situation or relationship where you
  were victimized. _____
  _____
  _____
  _____

- List things you do for others that indicate you are trying to rescue them. _____
  _____
  _____
  _____

We are either super-responsible or super-irresponsible. We try to solve others' problems or expect others to be responsible for us. This enables us to avoid looking closely at our own behavior.

- Describe those areas of your life in which you feel either super-responsible or super-irresponsible. _____

_____

_____

_____

We feel guilty when we stand up for ourselves or act assertively. We give in to others instead of taking care of ourselves.

- Identify recent situations in which you were afraid to express your desires or feelings and, instead, gave in to others. _____

_____

_____

_____

We deny, minimize or repress our feelings from our traumatic childhoods. We lose the ability to express our feelings and are unaware of the impact this has on our lives.

- How do you express your feelings and acknowledge them when something is upsetting you in your work or relationships? _____

_____

_____

_____

We are dependent personalities who are terrified of rejection or abandonment. We tend to stay in jobs or relationships that are harmful to us. Our fears can either stop us from ending hurtful relationships or prevent us from entering into healthy, rewarding ones.

- In which of your present relationships do you fear rejection or abandonment? _____

_____

_____

_____

- How do you deal with this fear? _____

_____

_____

_____

Denial, isolation, control and misplaced guilt are symptoms of family dysfunction. As a result of these behaviors, we feel hopeless and helpless.

- Having been a victim of family dysfunction, describe which symptoms are most prevalent? _____

_____

_____

_____

We have difficulty with intimate relationships. We feel insecure and lack trust in others. We don't have clearly defined boundaries and become enmeshed with our partner's needs and emotions.

- Describe your present difficulties with intimate relationships. _____

_____

_____

_____

We have difficulty following projects through from beginning to end.

- Describe projects you have started and have not completed from lack of motivation or procrastination. _____

_____

_____

_____

We have a strong need to be in control. We over-react to change over which we have no control.

- What do you fear most when you are not in control? _____

_____

_____

_____

STEP ONE

We admitted we were powerless over the effects of our separation from God—that our lives had become unmanageable.

I know that nothing good lives in me, that is, in my sinful nature.
For I have the desire to do what is good, but I cannot carry it out.
(Romans 7:18)

The ideas presented in Step One are overwhelming to most of us until we begin to see our lives as they really are. It is threatening to imagine that we could be powerless, and that our lives could be unmanageable. Our life experiences, however, remind us that our behavior does not always produce peace and serenity. Our background, if affected by alcohol or other types of family dysfunction, subverts our highest intentions, motivations and ambitions. In many cases, it has caused a separation from God. Although it is often not our intention, frequently our behavior is not what we want it to be.

We may have been taught to believe that all we have to do is accept Christ as our Lord and Savior for our lives to be complete and satisfying. This may have been the magic we relied upon to prepare us for the here and hereafter. Our proclamation that "I am born anew; the past is washed clean; I am a new creature; Christ has totally changed me" may be helping us to deny the actual condition of our lives. Grace in God's sight is achieved the moment we accept Christ into our lives. Achieving the condition of reconciliation, however, is an ongoing life-long process.

The fact that we still feel pain from our past is not a sign of a failed relationship with God, nor does it lessen the impact of salvation in our lives. This is simply a signal we need to continue the process of working the Steps and praying, looking to God to make the necessary changes. This acknowledgment may seem to be a contradiction of our strong claim to salvation, but it is not. The Bible is full of accounts of men and women who struggled continually to overcome past mistakes, the weaknesses of their human nature and life's many temptations.

The idea that there are areas of our lives over which we are powerless is a new concept for us. It is much easier for us to feel that we have power and are in control of our lives. Paul the Apostle, in his letter to the Church of Rome, describes his desperate powerlessness and the unmanageability of his life. He writes of his continued sinful behavior as a manifestation of his separation from God. (Romans 7:14) His acknowledgment of this does not interfere with his commitment to do God's will. Without knowing the details of Paul's background, we can only assume that his self-will was a detriment to his functioning effectively in his life. Because of our background, we function in much the same way as Paul did, allowing our self-will to work against us. We do have the power to choose to look to God, and exercising this choice will be enabled by our work in Step Two.

We live in a culture that places a high value on individual accomplishment. Most of us, from the time we were small children, were bombarded by the ideal of high achievement. Competition for grades, high achievement in sports and competitiveness in business are all viewed as the norm in our society. They are considered to be measures of success. We are taught that if we compete hard enough we will be "winners" and, therefore, good people. If, however, we fail to measure up to what is expected of us and are "losers," we will be bad people. Due to the absence of appropriate role models in childhood, many of us are confused as to where we fit in. We continue to allow our worth and self-esteem to be determined by what we do and what others think of us, and not by who we are in Christ. Looking back at our past, we may continue to classify ourselves as "losers," and to condition ourselves to fail. Our low self-esteem keeps us from becoming "winners." Living in this environment creates extreme stress and anxiety.

As we mature, matters get worse. The stressful lives we lead give us no satisfaction, and compound the problems. Our fears and insecurities increase, creating a sense of panic. Some of us revert to abusing mood-altering substances such as drugs, alcohol or food in order to relieve the tension resulting from our condition. In more subtle ways, we may bury ourselves in church activities, work, relationships or other addictive/compulsive behaviors to try to combat the anxieties that exist in our lives. When we come to grips with ourselves and realize that our lives are just one big roller-coaster ride, we are ready for Step One. We have no alternative but to admit that we are powerless and that our lives have become unmanageable. When we begin to recognize the seriousness of our condition, it is important that we seek help.

Step One forms the foundation for working the other Steps. In this vital encounter with the circumstances of our lives, we admit our powerlessness and accept the unmanageability of our lives. Surrendering to this idea is not an easy thing to do. Although our behavior has caused us nothing but stress and pain, it is difficult to let go and trust that things will work out well. We may experience confusion, drowsiness, sadness, sleeplessness or turmoil. These are normal responses to the severe inner struggles we are experiencing. It is important to remember that surrender requires great mental and emotional energy and determination.

Personal Reflection

In Step One, we come to grips with the reality of our lives and ourselves. Perhaps for the first time, we finally admit defeat and recognize that we need help. In looking at Step One, we see it has two distinct parts: (1) the admission that we have obsessive traits and try to manipulate the affairs of our lives in order to ease the inner pain of separateness from God; that we are in the grip of an addictive process that has rendered us powerless over our behavior; and (2) the admission that our lives have been, and will continue to be, unmanageable if we insist on living by our own will.

- What difficulties are you having in recognizing your powerlessness and your life's unmanageability? _____

_____

_____

_____

PSALM 6:6-7
I am worn out from groaning; all night long I flood my bed with weeping and drench my couch with tears. My eyes grow weak with sorrow; they fail because of all my foes.

● What area of your life is causing you the most sadness? _____

_____

_____

_____

◆ ◆ ◆

Our instinct cries out against the idea of personal powerlessness and the fact that we are not in control. We have been accustomed to accepting full responsibility for all that happens in our lives as well as in the lives of others. Having been raised in a dysfunctional environment, it is natural for us to have some reaction. Some of us take on the role of being super-responsible while others of us withdraw and become super-irresponsible. Until we reach an intolerable threshold of pain, we will be unable to take the first step toward liberation and renewed strength. The fact that we are powerless is a truth we must realize before we can totally surrender.

● In what areas of your life have you exhibited the most destructive behavior? _____

_____

_____

_____

● What major event in your life has caused you to realize the extent of your pain?

_____

_____

_____

DEUTERONOMY 30:19-20
> *This day I call heaven and earth as witnesses against you that I have set before you life and death, blessings and curses. Now choose life, so that you and your children may live and that you may love the Lord your God, listen to his voice, and hold fast to him.*

● How can recognizing your pain and accepting powerlessness enable you to "choose life?"

_____

_____

_____

◆ ◆ ◆

As we begin to accept the reality of our condition, we naturally look to others for answers. We feel like timid spiritual beginners and wonder why the quality of life we were seeking has escaped us. Friends may tell us to read our Bible or "pray about it." Some may suggest we talk with our minister. No matter how many outside sources we seek, there will be no relief for us until we, by ourselves, in our own minds and hearts, acknowledge our powerlessness. Then, and only then, will we begin to see that Step One is the beginning of a way out.

● Why is it necessary for you to believe that you, on your own, are powerless? _____

_____

_____

_____

1 CORINTHIANS 8:2
The man who thinks he knows something does not yet know as he ought to know.

● How has thinking your life is working blocked you from seeing the reality of your problem? _____

_____

_____

_____

◆ ◆ ◆

Step One is not a once-and-for-all commitment. We must remember that our old traits, habits and behavior patterns are still with us. They are unconscious reactions to the common stresses of life. We must continually monitor our behavior and watch for the appearance of destructive tendencies. If we then admit our powerlessness and seek God's help, new courses of action will open up for us.

● In what area of your life do you experience the strongest need to be in control? _____

_____

_____

_____

● What are the consequences of your self-destructive habits? _____

_____

_____

_____

MARK 4:35-41
That day when evening came, he said to his disciples, "Let us go over to the other side." Leaving the crowd behind, they took him along, just as he was, in the boat. A furious squall came up, and the waves broke over the boat, so that it was nearly swamped. Jesus was in the stern, sleeping on a cushion. The disciples woke him and said to him, "Teacher, don't you care if we drown?"

He got up, rebuked the wind and said to the waves, "Quiet! Be still." Then the wind died down and it was completely calm. He said to his disciples, "Why are you so afraid? Do you still have no faith?" They were terrified and asked each other, "Who is this? Even the wind and the waves obey him."

● The Apostles felt fear and lack of trust as a result of their powerlessness. How do you experience fear and lack of trust as contributing to your feeling of powerlessness? _____

_____

_____

_____

◆ ◆ ◆

The second part of Step One, admitting that our lives are unmanageable, is equally as difficult as admitting that we are powerless. We can come to terms with this by continually observing all the things we have used in the past to hide the truth about ourselves. We need to be totally honest in order to drop the disguises and see things as they really are. When we stop finding excuses for our behavior, we will have taken the first step toward achieving the humility we need to accept spiritual guidance. It is through this spiritual guidance that we can begin to rebuild ourselves and our lives.

● In what area of your life do you experience the greatest sense of unmanageability? ____

_____

_____

_____

● Cite specific situations wherein you find excuses for your behavior. _____

_____

_____

_____

JOHN 15:1-8

"I am the true vine and my Father is the gardener. He cuts off every branch in me that bears no fruit, while every branch that does bear fruit he trims clean so that it will be even more fruitful. You are already clean because of the word I have spoken to you. Remain in me, and I will remain in you. No branch can bear fruit by itself; it must remain in the vine. Neither can you bear fruit unless you remain in me."

"I am the vine; you are the branches. If a man remains in me and I in him, he will bear much fruit; apart from me you can do nothing. If anyone does not remain in me, he is like a branch that is thrown away and withers; such branches are picked up, thrown into the fire and burned. If you remain in me and my words remain in you, ask whatever you wish, and it will be given you. This is to my Father's glory, that you bear much fruit, showing yourselves to be my disciples."

● Which non-productive behaviors of your life need to be eliminated? _____

_____

_____

_____

◆ ◆ ◆

Just as the healing of a physical disease can only begin when we acknowledge the disease, so the spiritual healing of our obsessive/compulsive behavior begins when we acknowledge the existence of the problem. In Mark 10:51, it was obvious to others that Bartimaeus was blind. However, he had to openly *ask* Christ to heal his blindness. Until we realize this truth, our progress toward recovery will be blocked. Our healing begins when we are willing to acknowledge our problems.

● What behavior do you have that is difficult to acknowledge as being a problem? _____

_____

_____

_____

LUKE 15:17

When he came to his senses, he said, "How many of my father's hired men have food to spare, and here I am starving to death!"

- The prodigal son's decision to live a self-centered life rendered him powerless and caused his life to become unmanageable. In what ways are you like the prodigal son? _____

_____

_____

_____

◆ ◆ ◆

As we progress through the Steps, we will discover that true and lasting change does not happen by trying to alter our life conditions. Although it is tempting to think so, exterior adjustments cannot correct the problem that exists within us. Deep and profound healing requires surrendering the belief that we can heal our lives by manipulating our environment. Our willingness to work the Steps will enable us to begin our true healing, which must begin on the inside.

- In the past, how have you tried to alter your life conditions by manipulating your environment? _____

_____

_____

_____

ROMANS 7:18-20

> *"I know that nothing good lives in me, that is, in my sinful nature. For I have the desire to do what is good, but I cannot carry it out. For what I do is not the good I want to do; no, the evil I do not want to do—this I keep on doing. Now if I do what I do not want to do, it is no longer I who do it, but it is sin living in me that does it."*

- List examples that indicate you have a desire to do what is good, but cannot carry it out.

_____

_____

_____

◆ ◆ ◆

As we work toward complete and ongoing recovery, we become aware that we are not alone. Our Lord has said He will not leave us comfortless. As we grow in faith, we will come to know His constant presence. To the degree that we desire to increase our spiritual strength, it will grow. Eternal vigilance is necessary so that we do not slip back into our old behaviors. Each day is a new opportunity to admit our powerlessness and our unmanageability.

- How does the Lord comfort you and help you accept the powerlessness and unmanageability of your life? _____

_____

_____

_____

2 CORINTHIANS 12:9-10

> *But he said to me, "My grace is sufficient for you, for my power is made perfect in weakness." Therefore I will boast all the more gladly about my weaknesses, so that Christ's power may rest on me. That is why, for Christ's sake, I delight in weaknesses, in insults, in hardships, in persecutions, in difficulties. For when I am weak, then I am strong.*

● What does "for when I am weak, then I am strong" mean to you? _____

_____

_____

_____

♦ ♦ ♦

As we begin our journey toward recovery by working the Twelve Steps, old truths will have new meaning for us. We will know what it means when we say we can never be separated from the love of God. Our faith in God, and our renewed emerging faith in ourselves and others, will sustain us as we experience the inevitable pain and suffering that our rigorous self-examination will cause. It is the only way out for us; the only way to a new life in Christ.

● What are your fears concerning the pain and suffering you may experience as a result of self-examination? _____

_____

_____

_____

PROVERBS 28:26

> *He who trusts in himself is a fool, but he who walks in wisdom is kept safe.*

● Why is trusting yourself not a wise thing to do? _____

_____

_____

_____

♦ ♦ ♦

Notes: _____

_____

_____

_____

_____

_____

_____

_____

_____

Notes: _____

_____

_____

_____

_____

_____

_____

_____

_____

_____

_____

_____

_____

_____

_____

_____

_____

_____

_____

_____

_____

_____

_____

_____

_____

_____

_____

_____

_____

_____

_____

_____

STEP TWO

Came to believe that a power greater than ourselves
could restore us to sanity.

For it is God who works in you to will and
to act according to his good purpose.
(Philippians 2:13)

Having come to grips with the fact that we are powerless and our lives are unmanageable, our next step is to acknowledge the existence of a Power greater than ourselves. Believing in God does not always mean that we accept His Power. As Christians, we know God, but do not necessarily invite His Power into our lives. In Step Two, we have an opportunity to experience God in a different light. As Jesus asserted in John 14:26, the Holy Spirit will be sent in His name, to teach us and remind us of all He has taught. Here we begin to re-establish our relationship, or, establish a relationship with God for the first time. The purpose of this Step is to show us that He is a Power greater than ourselves and a vital part of our daily lives.

For many of us, this Step presents major problems. The aloneness of our present condition demands that we depend on our own resources. We do not trust ourselves or others. We may even doubt that God can heal us or, indeed, even be interested in doing so. Unless we let go of our distrust and begin to lean on God, we will continue to operate in an insane manner. The chaos and confusion of our lives will only increase.

Depending on our religious background, some of us may have been taught that God is an authority to be feared. We have never come to know Him as a loving God. As children, we were very anxious and fearful of doing something wrong. The threat of being punished by God was used by adults to control our childish behavior. Our fear of displeasing God magnified our growing sense of guilt and shame. As adults, we continue to fear people in authority and are often overcome by guilt and shame for simple misdeeds.

We still may be harboring childhood anger at God, because He disappointed us many times. Due to the severity of our experiences, some of us have rejected God because He did not give us relief from our pain. Despite our conviction that God is with us, in moments of fear we doubt His presence. Even those who are coming to terms with their problems, and are in contact with their Higher Power, experience moments of doubt. In Step Two, our goal is to fully accept the presence and guidance of God, in order to begin the journey to peace and serenity.

For some of us, belief in self-will and our ability to manage our own lives is all we have. We perceive God as a crutch for children and weak-willed individuals who are incapable of managing their own lives. As we begin to see the true nature of God, a weight is lifted from our shoulders, and we begin to view life from a different perspective.

One of the great paradoxes of Christianity is that man is never completely free until he has become totally submissive. In John 8:32, Jesus made a promise when he said, "You shall know the truth and the truth shall make you free." In this Step, we begin to recognize that

God does, in fact, have the power and intention to alter the course of our lives. In the scriptures, we are assured of God's presence within us. We are shown beyond all doubt that through Him all things are possible. If you have accepted the truth regarding your condition and are ready to surrender to your Higher Power, you are well on your way to ultimate submission and true spiritual freedom.

Step Two is referred to as the Hope Step. It gives us new hope as we begin to see that help is available to us if we simply reach out and accept what Jesus Christ, our Higher Power has to offer. It is here that we form the foundation for growth of our spiritual life, which will help us become the person we want to be. All that is required of us is a willingness to believe that a Power greater than ourselves is waiting to be our personal savior. What follows as we proceed through the Steps is a process that will bring this Power into our lives and enable us to grow in love, health and grace.

Personal Reflection

Coming to believe in a Power greater than ourselves requires faith. In the past, we have placed our faith in our own abilities to run our lives, and that faith has proven worthless. It was misplaced and could never have done for us what we thought it would. Now we need to actively place our faith in Jesus Christ (Romans 10:8-10). At first, it may seem unrealistic to place our faith in a Power we cannot see or touch. Yet the very existence of our universe in all its glory gives ample evidence of the true power, love and majesty of the God we seek.

- List some of the experiences that caused you to lose faith in God. _____
  _____
  _____
  _____

- How can faith help you accept and trust in a Power greater than yourself? _____
  _____
  _____
  _____

MATTHEW 14:22-34

Immediately Jesus made the disciples get into the boat and go on ahead of him to the other side, while he dismissed the crowd. After he had dismissed them, he went up into the hills by himself to pray. When evening came, he was there alone, but the boat was already a considerable distance from land, buffeted by the waves because the wind was against it. During the fourth watch of the night Jesus went out to them, walking on the lake. When the disciples saw him walking on the lake, they were terrified. "It's a ghost," they said, and cried out in fear. But Jesus immediately said to them: "Take courage! It is I. Don't be afraid." "Lord, if it's you," Peter replied, "tell me to come to you on the water." "Come," he said. Then Peter got down out of the boat and walked on the water to Jesus. But when he saw the wind, he was afraid and, beginning to sink, cried out, "Lord, save me!" Immediately Jesus reached out his hand and caught him. "You of little faith," he said, "why did you doubt?" And when they climbed into the boat, the wind died down. Then those who were in the boat worshiped him, saying, "Truly you are the Son of God."

- How does Peter's experience illustrate that the belief in a Power greater than yourself will give you strength? _____

_____

_____

_____

◆ ◆ ◆

Faith grows through practice. Each time we state a conviction and prove it by our actions, our faith becomes stronger. Every time we ask Christ, our Higher Power for help, we will receive it, and our faith will be strengthened. We will finally accept the fact that He is dependable and will never leave us. All we need to do is ask for help and trust in His Power.

- List recent events or situations that indicate your faith is being strengthened. _____

_____

_____

_____

MATTHEW 17:20

He replied, "Because you have so little faith. I tell you the truth, if you have faith as small as a mustard seed, you can say to this mountain, 'Move from here to there' and it will move. Nothing will be impossible for you."

- What is an example of your having "faith as small as a mustard seed?" _____

_____

_____

_____

MARK 9:23-24

"'If you can'?" said Jesus. "Everything is possible for him who believes." Immediately the boy's father exclaimed, "I do believe; help me overcome my unbelief!"

- What is keeping you from truly believing that a Power greater than yourself can restore you to sanity? _____

_____

_____

_____

◆ ◆ ◆

One of the greatest secrets of learning to have faith is found in the joyful revelation that the Spirit of God is always available. His greatest desire is that He might share that kind of relationship with us. He can and will be as close to us as we allow Him to be.

- Describe your personal relationship with God. _____

_____

_____

_____

PSALM 34:18-22

The Lord is close to the brokenhearted and saves those who are crushed in spirit. A righteous man may have many troubles, but the Lord delivers him from them all; he protects all his bones, not one of them will be broken. Evil will slay the wicked; the foe of the righteous will be condemned. The Lord redeems his servants; no one who takes refuge in him will be condemned.

● How can your relationship with Jesus Christ help mend your crushed and broken spirit?

_____

_____

_____

◆ ◆ ◆

As we develop a relationship with Jesus Christ as our Higher Power, we begin to rely on Him to help us become aware of the extent of our disabling condition. Step Two implies that we are insane. The dictionary defines insanity as "inability to manage one's own affairs and perform one's social duties...without recognition of one's own illness." In this sense, we can see our behavior as insane. We still may be blaming everyone and everything for our condition instead of taking responsibility for our own behavior.

● Describe your inability to manage your own affairs. _____

_____

_____

_____

2 CORINTHIANS 1:9

Indeed, in our hearts we felt the sentence of death. But this happened that we might not rely on ourselves but on God, who raises the dead.

● How and where in your heart have you felt certain you would die before your time?

_____

_____

_____

◆ ◆ ◆

Because of our traumatic childhood experiences, we have become defiant, indifferent, resentful, self-deluded and self-centered. These conditions indicate that our lives need to be restored to a more balanced state. We can do this if we are willing to believe that a Power greater than ourselves can restore us to sanity. If we attempt to do it alone, we easily can deceive ourselves by looking to outside sources for the causes of our disability. With the help of Christ, we will heal these deceitful behaviors.

● Which of the above conditions have caused you to behave inappropriately? Explain. ____

_____

_____

_____

PHILIPPIANS 2:13
  For it is God who works in you to will and to act according to his good purpose.

● How do you see God restoring you to sanity? _____

_____

_____

_____

◆ ◆ ◆

One of the ways in which Christ helps us see our condition clearly is by bringing us into contact with others who have had experiences similar to ours. It becomes evident, when sharing our stories, that each of us can maintain "emotional sobriety" only one day at a time. We soon see that all worry, depression, compulsions and obsessions are unhealthy. The fact that we ever believed we could control ourselves without help from our Higher Power was insane. He helps us realize that actions which are destructive to ourselves or to others are not acceptable. As we become more dependent on our Higher Power, the quality of our lives will improve.

● How do depressions, compulsions and obsessions interfere with your ability to function

normally? _____

_____

_____

_____

● What can you do to maintain your "emotional sobriety?" _____

_____

_____

_____

2 CORINTHIANS 3:5
  Not that we are competent to claim anything for ourselves, but our competence comes from God.

● How does your relationship with God improve your competence in dealing with your

life? _____

_____

_____

_____

◆ ◆ ◆

When we started this program, we may have been expecting instant results. From our childhood, we remember feeling anger or confusion when things didn't happen "right now." In this program, sudden change is the exception, not the rule. It requires patience and perseverance to achieve the recovery we seek. Each of us is unique, and recovery begins for each of us at different stages in the Steps. Some of us may experience instant relief, whereas others may not begin to feel stronger until later in the Program. There is no rule or guideline. Your progress will occur at the appropriate time for you.

- What is your reaction to the fact that recovery requires patience and understanding, that it doesn't happen instantly? _____

_____

_____

_____

ISAIAH 40:28-31

Do you not know? Have you not heard? The Lord is the everlasting God, the Creator of the ends of the earth. He will not grow tired or weary, and his understanding no one can fathom. He gives strength to the weary and increases the power of the weak. Even youths grow tired and weary, and young men stumble and fall; but those who hope in the Lord will renew their strength. They will soar on wings like eagles; they will run and not grow weary, they will walk and not be faint.

- How does the Lord, as your Higher Power, help renew your strength? _____

_____

_____

_____

♦ ♦ ♦

Step Two promises a restoration to sanity. Allowing this state of mind to unfold requires humility. Humility grows within a gentle and nurturing character, without pride and aggressiveness. For most of us, lack of humility contributed to our present situation. Developing humility is a recurrent theme of the Program. We become humble as we are slowly able to relinquish our pride. In Philippians 2:5 we are told, "Your attitude should be the same as that of Christ Jesus."

- In what areas of your life do you demonstrate aggressiveness? _____

_____

_____

_____

- In what aspects of your life do you need to be more gentle and nurturing? _____

_____

_____

_____

ROMANS 8:38-39

For I am convinced that neither death nor life, neither angels nor demons, neither height nor depth, nor anything else in all creation, will be able to separate us from the love of God that is in Christ Jesus our Lord.

- What is your relationship with Jesus Christ? How can it be improved? _____

_____

_____

_____

♦ ♦ ♦

When we become ready to accept fully our powerlessness and unmanageability (Step One), when we accept Jesus Christ, our Higher Power and our insanity (Step Two), we will be ready to take action and turn our lives over to the care of God (Step Three). There is no need to rush the process of working the Steps. The important thing is to heed the Bible's admonition ''the hour has come for you to wake up from your slumber.'' (Romans 13:11) Move forward in faith so you will be able to proceed with the remaining Steps.

- List areas in Step One or Step Two where you are still having difficulty inviting Christ into your life. _____

  _____

  _____

  _____

- What can you do to remedy this problem? _____

  _____

  _____

  _____

ISAIAH 41:10

So do not fear for I am with you; do not be dismayed, for I am your God. I will strengthen and help you; I will uphold you with my righteous right hand.

- What help do you want from the Lord as you begin to look to him for strength? _____

  _____

  _____

  _____

JOHN 3:16-17

For God so loved the world that he gave his one and only Son, that whoever believes in him shall not perish but have eternal life. For God did not send his Son into the world to condemn the world, but to save the world through him.

- How do you see the Twelve Steps as effective tools for gaining the "fullness of life" that God has promised us? _____

  _____

  _____

  _____

♦ ♦ ♦

Notes: _____

_____

_____

_____

_____

_____

_____

_____

_____

_____

_____

_____

_____

_____

_____

_____

_____

_____

_____

_____

_____

_____

_____

_____

_____

_____

_____

_____

_____

_____

_____

_____

_____

_____

_____

STEP THREE

*Made a decision to turn our will and our lives over
to the care of God as we understood Him.*

> *Therefore, I urge you, brothers, in view of God's mercy,
> to offer your bodies as living sacrifices, holy and pleasing
> to God—which is your spiritual worship.*
>
> (Romans 12:1)

Step Three is the central theme of all the Steps. It is the point at which we make a decision to turn our will and our lives over to the care of God. Step Three is an important cornerstone for building an effective and peaceful life. In Steps One and Two we established the basis for turning our lives over to the care of God. The commitment we now make in Step Three must be repeated more than once, for actually we are just beginning to turn things over to God. Repeated working of the first three Steps helps to build a solid foundation for working the total program.

Many of us come to this program with strong negative perceptions about the world in which we live. They may be based on hurtful childhood experiences, unprincipled academic training or simply the accumulated lessons of our lives. As a result of other experiences from our past, we may have understood God to be unloving and judgmental. Whatever the source, our recovery is hindered if our beliefs make it difficult to let go of our fear and surrender our lives to God. If we have experienced extreme violence as children, we may be resistant to risk trusting anyone or anything—even God. In Step Three, we decide to take the leap of faith and put our lives in His hands.

Biblical figures often resisted following God's will. The Bible illustrates some examples of doing God's will when it didn't make any sense. Yet, the end result demonstrated it was wise to follow God's guidance. Acts of faith are exemplified by Moses leading the Jewish people out of the wilderness; by Abraham's willingness to sacrifice his son Isaac. Also, despite criticism of his contemporaries, Noah built the ark. The essence of these actions is summarized in Hebrews 11:6; "And without faith it is impossible to please God, because anyone who comes to Him must believe that He exists and that He rewards those who earnestly seek Him."

Until now, our inaccurate perceptions of reality have led us into many compulsive/obsessive behaviors. Admitting our responsibility for these dysfunctions is too difficult. It implies that we have not been "good people." Denial is our only recourse. Our denial acts as a shield against confronting ourselves as we really are. When denial is at work, it is like a shuttered window, closing out the sunlight. In Step Three, we begin the process of opening the shutters and allowing the light to enter. Our trust in God is a source of light with which we can examine our behavior.

Step Three is an affirmative step. It is time to make a decision. In the first two Steps, we became aware of our condition and accepted the idea of a Power greater than ourselves. Although we began to know and trust Him, we may find it difficult to think of allowing God to be totally in charge of our lives. However, if the alternative is facing the loss of something critical to our existence, such as family, job, health or sanity, God's guidance might be easier to accept. Right now our lives may have many beautiful and rewarding relationships which are being ruined by our addictive/compulsive behavior. We must not be discouraged by these discoveries. Our healing work continues in Step Four where we identify our dysfunctions. Remember, it takes relentless courage to search out our weaknesses and turn everything over to God for healing.

As we begin to allow God's will to act in our lives, our self-destructive tendencies become weaker and much less distracting. Often, the confusion and grief we cause ourselves and others prevent us from successfully working and practicing the Steps. Making the decision to begin this journey to health is an act of great importance and should not be made in a time of emotional upheaval. Turning our lives over means consciously relinquishing our destructive self-will and our compulsive behaviors, as well as our talents, potentialities, skills and ambitions. The key elements here are making the decision with a clear and rational mind, being committed to that decision and, finally, trusting the outcome to God.

As we surrender our lives and stop carrying the burdens of our past, we will begin to feel better about ourselves. The more we learn to trust in the Lord, the more we will trust ourselves and extend that trust to others. Our decision to choose God's way will restore us to fullness of life. As we free ourselves from our negative behaviors, we will deal more effectively with the daily routine of our lives. Our impatience and irritability disappear as we come to know His love and yearn to share it with others. Our lives transform into a lived-out relationship with God, and we will become the persons He meant for us to be—workers in His kingdom.

Personal Reflection

In Step Three, we make an important decision. It is time to acknowledge our need for God's presence in our lives, and to give ourselves to Him. We make the decision to surrender our lives to God. He becomes our new manager, and we accept life on His terms. He offers us a way to live that is free from the emotional pollution of our past, thereby allowing us to enjoy new and wonderful experiences. Step Three provides us with an opportunity to turn away from behavior that fosters addiction, discouragement, sickness and fear.

• Describe your readiness to make the decision to turn your life over to the care of God.

_____

_____

_____

PROVERBS 3:5-6
  Trust in the Lord with all your heart and lean not on your own understanding; in all your ways acknowledge him, and he will make your paths straight.

• How do you expect the Lord to help you make your paths straight? _____

_____

_____

_____

PSALM 143: 10-11
> *Teach me to do your will, for you are my God; may your good Spirit lead me on level ground.*

● How can the Holy Spirit help you accept life on God's terms? _____

_____

_____

_____

◆ ◆ ◆

Many of us begin this Step Three process by deciding to turn over only certain parts of our lives. We are willing to surrender the most difficult problems when we see they are making our lives unmanageable. We cling to other areas of our lives because we think we can manage them. We eventually realize that we cannot barter with God. We must be prepared to surrender our entire will and every part of our lives to His care in order to recover. When we are truly able to accept this fact, our journey to wholeness has begun.

● Which parts of your life are you most willing to turn over to God? _____

_____

_____

_____

● Which parts of your life are you most unwilling to turn over to God? How does willfullness prevent you from giving them up? _____

_____

_____

_____

ROMANS 12:1
> *Therefore, I urge you, brothers, in view of God's mercy, to offer your bodies as living sacrifices, holy and pleasing to God—which is your spiritual worship.*

● How will offering your life to God help to reduce the stress in your life. _____

_____

_____

_____

◆ ◆ ◆

Step Three may make us feel we are losing our identity. We may feel we are going to lose everything. Not knowing what is going to happen is frightening. Most of us have tried desperately to control our environment. Many of these behavior traits were developed during childhood and came about as a direct result of the atmosphere in which we were raised. Deep within us may be a fearful and trembling child, anxious about someone's anger, criticism, threats or violence. As children, we tried to fix or take care of the people around us so they would not abandon us, leaving only broken promises and shattered dreams.

● How do your childhood memories continue to frighten you? _____

_____

_____

_____

JOHN 1:12-13

Yet to all who received him, to those who believed in his name, he gave the right to become children of God—children born not of natural descent, nor of human decision or a husband's will, but born of God.

● How would you describe your childhood relationship with God? _____

_____

_____

_____

◆ ◆ ◆

The conditions in which we were raised often kept us from ever having trust in God. Our prayers may have been unanswered, and we could not imagine how a loving God could be so cruel to us. Step Three is an opportunity to start over. As we work the Steps and get in touch with the forgotten child within us, we see that God's healing love will repair the damage that has been done. Jesus told us that we must become like children to enter the Kingdom of God. This statement helps us recognize that a childlike state will enable us to regain our capacity to give and receive unconditonal love. With this in mind, we can look forward to getting in touch with the child within us, who so desperately wants to give and receive love and nurturing.

● How can Step Three be an opportunity to start over and repair your relationship with

your forgotten child? _____

_____

_____

_____

MATTHEW 11:28-30

"Come to me, all you who are weary and burdened, and I will give you rest. Take my yoke upon you and learn from me, for I am gentle and humble in heart, and you will find rest for your souls. For my yoke is easy and my burden is light."

● How will coming to the Lord for guidance lighten your burden?

_____

_____

_____

◆ ◆ ◆

Learning to trust in God and accept His support will enhance greatly the quality of our lives. We will no longer feel the need to carry our burdens by ourselves. Much of the pain of our past is a result of feeling totally alone. With His presence, our sense of self-esteem will improve, and we will begin to recognize that we are worthwhile human beings. Our capacity to receive and give love will increase, and we will come to place great value on fellowship and sharing.

- How will you know when your self-esteem begins to improve? _____

_____

_____

_____

PSALM 118:8-9

It is better to take refuge in the Lord than to trust in man. It is better to take refuge in the Lord than to trust in princes.

- Where has trusting in man failed you? _____

_____

_____

_____

◆ ◆ ◆

Christ exemplifies "turning it over" by acceptance of the will of His Father, which led to the Cross and the victory of resurrection. During His life on earth, Jesus' love for us led him into constant confrontations with the forces of evil. He was strong and steadfast because He placed His trust in His Heavenly Father. We, too, will be strong in the face of trial and temptation because we know that God, our Heavenly Father, will never abandon us.

- Identify ways in which you relate to Christ's willingness to do His Father's will. _____

_____

_____

_____

MATTHEW 26:30

Going a little farther, he fell with his face to the ground and prayed, "My Father, if it is possible, may this cup be taken from me. Yet not as I will, but as you will."

- How does this incident in the life of Christ represent practicing Step Three? _____

_____

_____

_____

◆ ◆ ◆

In this life, we also have crosses to bear. Some of us still may be experiencing the powerful impact of our history of disabling behavior. Whatever our addiction may be—drugs, destructive relationships, sex, alcohol, money or food—we face the possibility of spiritual as well as physical death. As we turn away from these temptations, we accept God's offer to cast our burdens upon Him.

- What cross are you currently carrying that turns you to God for guidance? _____

_____

_____

_____

GALATIANS 2:20

> *I have been crucified with Christ and I no longer live, but Christ lives in me. The life I live in the body, I live by faith in the Son of God, who loved me and gave himself for me.*

- What is your experience of Christ living in you? How does His presence help you cope

  with your daily life? _____

_____

_____

_____

◆ ◆ ◆

It is important to remember that, as we practice Step Three on a daily basis, we will see a change come over us. We will be calmer, and will no longer feel responsible for everything and everybody. Peace and serenity will come to us in measures never before experienced. Our eyes will be opened, and we will have a fresh start in life. We will become increasingly aware that God is guiding us. People around us may notice that we have become more confident and trustworthy.

- What changes have you seen in yourself that can be attributed to working the Steps?

_____

_____

_____

PROVERBS 16:3

> *Commit to the Lord whatever you do, and your plans will succeed.*

- Why is it possible for plans to succeed by committing them to the Lord? _____

_____

_____

_____

◆ ◆ ◆

No matter how far we progress in recovery, we must continually turn our lives over to the care of God and be vigilant. It is foolish for us not to anticipate relapses. We need only to recognize this, and to be willing to work the Program on a daily basis. It is especially important to continue to practice Step Three. Our willingness to trust in God ensures our victory.

- How do you plan to practice Step Three in your daily routine of living? _____

_____

_____

_____

JOHN 14:12-13

I tell you the truth, anyone who has faith in me will do what I have been doing. He will do even greater things than these, because I am going to the Father. And I will do whatever you ask in my name, so that the Son may bring glory to the Father.

● How do you see your life improving because of your decision to surrender to God's will?

_____

_____

_____

JEREMIAH 29:11-14

"For I know the plans I have for you," declares the Lord, "plans to prosper you and not to harm you, plans to give you hope and a future. Then you will call upon me and come and pray to me, and I will listen to you. You will seek me and find me when you seek me with all your heart. I will be found by you," declares the Lord."

● What kind of loving attention can we expect to receive when we turn ourselves over to

God's care? _____

_____

_____

_____

◆ ◆ ◆

The path you are about to take has been walked by countless thousands of people seeking to experience peace, serenity and companionship with the Lord. Our daily task is to continually ask God for guidance. We receive Christ by personal invitation. "Here I am! I stand at the door and knock. If anyone hears my voice and opens the door, I will come in and eat with him, and he with me." (Revelations 3:20)

Reciting the following prayer can strengthen us in our daily walk.

STEP THREE PRAYER

Lord Jesus, I turn my life over to you,
to mold me and do with me as you will.
Trusting that you guide my steps,
I enter the world with hope;
that I may better do your will.
I welcome your Holy Spirit's Power, Love
and Guidance in everything I do."
Amen.

SPIRITUAL LOG

As part of our spiritual walk with the Lord, it is helpful to maintain a log of our meaningful experiences with Christ.

The following pages are intended to be used for recording these experiences during your Spiritual Journey toward wholeness.

_____

_____

_____

_____

_____

_____

_____

_____

_____

_____

_____

_____

_____

_____

_____

_____

_____

_____

_____

_____

_____

_____

_____

_____

_____

_____

_____

_____

STEP FOUR

Made a searching and fearless moral inventory of ourselves.

*Let us examine our ways and test
them, and let us return to the Lord.*
(Lamentations 3:40)

Step Four begins the growth steps of our journey. Here, we examine our behavior and expand our understanding of ourselves. The adventure of self-discovery begins with Step Four and continues through Step Seven. During this time, we will prepare a personal inventory, discuss it with others in the Program and invite God to remove our shortcomings. Being totally honest in preparing our inventory is vital to the self-discovery that forms the foundation of our recovery. It allows us to remove the obstacles that have prevented us from knowing ourselves and truthfully acknowledging our deepest feelings about life.

Step Four helps us get in touch with our "shadow," that part of us which we have hidden away for so long—our repressed nature. In the process of making our inventory, we will develop and broaden our understanding of our behavior. We will see that our "shadow" is an integral part of our nature and must be accepted by us. This part of our nature hides our resentments, fears and other repressed feelings. As we reveal ourselves, our acceptance of our whole character will free us to discover that these behaviors, begun in childhood, provided us with the means of survival. In the context of our turbulent early years, these behaviors were life-saving; but their continuation into our adulthood renders us dysfunctional.

Denial is a key survival skill that we learned early in childhood. It stunted our emotional growth by keeping us in a make-believe world. We often fantasized that our situation was better than it really was. Denial protected us from our feelings and helped us repress the pain of our family environment. Our shame and guilt caused us to be silent, rather than be honest and face the fear of being ridiculed by others. This withdrawal hindered us from developing into mature, emotionally healthy adults. As our self-discovery unfolds, we begin to recognize the role that denial has played in our lives. This realization is the basis for our acceptance of the truth of our personal history.

Resentment and fear are two issues that need to be dealt with before we begin the process of preparing our inventory. Our resentment toward people, places and things that have injured us keeps us preoccupied and limits our ability to live in the present moment. Resentment results from hiding the bitter hurts that have tarnished our lives. It evokes anger, frustration and depression. When our resentments are unresolved, we risk developing severe physical and mental illnesses.

Fear limits our ability to be rational. When fear is present, it is difficult to see situations in their true perspective. Fear is the root of other repressive and painful feelings. It prevents us from expressing ourselves honestly and stops us from responding in appropriate ways to threatening situations. In order to change our behavior, we must first face and accept our fears. By acknowledging our fearful nature, we can expect a temporary loss of self-esteem, which will return as we become more willing to rely on God.

Preparing our inventory requires that we look to God for guidance. Having renewed our relationship in Steps Two and Three, we now ask God for help. We will be looking closely at our personal histories and acknowledge what we see there. Remembering that God is with us will make this task much easier. With God's help, we can courageously review our strengths and our weaknesses. As the process unfolds, we will begin to recognize the need for change.

Step Four gives us the opportunity to recognize that certain skills, acquired in childhood, may be inappropriate in our adult lives. Blaming others for our misfortunes, disclaiming responsibility for hurtful behavior and resisting the truth are behavior patterns we must discard. These certain learned behaviors were developed early in life and have become character defects. Looking at them now can be extremely troublesome. Painful memories may return, and we will remember things that we had thought were forgotten. Our willingness to be honest about what we uncover will give us the clarity of mind that is vital for our complete recovery.

Putting our thoughts on paper is valuable and necessary when completing Step Four. The process of writing focuses our wandering thoughts and allows us to concentrate on what is really happening. It often causes repressed feelings to surface and gives us a deeper understanding of ourselves and our behavior. Making our fearless moral inventory provides insights regarding our strengths and weaknesses. Rather than judge ourselves, we need to accept whatever we discover, knowing that this discovery is merely another step toward a healthy life. Successful completion of Step Four requires us to be honest and thorough. With God's help, and our personal courage, we can expect to receive limitless benefits.

Personal Reflection

Denial stems from our childhood environment, which we were unable to control. This was our reaction to the confusion, instability and violence of the care-taking adults around us. We rationalized what was happening and invented acceptable reasons for their unacceptable behavior. By doing this, we ignored the chaos and denied the insurmountable problems. As we matured, our denial continued to protect us from the need to face reality and helped us hide behind our delusions and fantasies.

- Cite examples that indicate you hide from reality. _____
  _____
  _____
  _____

JEREMIAH 17:9-10
> *"The heart is deceitful above all things and beyond cure. Who can understand it? I the Lord search the heart and examine the mind, to reward a man according to his conduct, according to what his deeds deserve."*

- How has your deceitful heart supported your ability to deny your condition? _____
  _____
  _____
  _____

♦ ♦ ♦

The power of denial is illustrated in the Bible when Peter denies Christ. Because of his great love for Him, Peter thought it inconceivable that he could deny Christ. However, when Peter was confronted with the situation, it was easier for him to deny Christ than it was to admit being a follower and face the consequences. When Peter realized what he had done, he was devastated. In much the same way, when we realize what denial has done to us, we will experience feelings of self-hatred, which need to be acknowledged and resolved.

● Describe areas of your life in which denial has been harmful to you. _____

_____

_____

_____

MARK 14:66-72

While Peter was below in the courtyard, one of the servant girls of the high priest came by. When she saw Peter warming himself, she looked closely at him. "you also were with that Nazarene, Jesus," she said. But he denied it. "I don't know or understand what you're talking about," he said, and went out into the entryway. When the servant girl saw him there, she said again to those standing around, "this fellow is one of them." Again he denied it. After a little while, those standing near said to Peter, "Surely you are one of them, for you are a Galilean." He began to call down curses on himself, and swore to them, "I don't know this man you're talking about." Immediately the rooster crowed the second time. Then Peter remembered the word Jesus had spoken to him: "Before the rooster crows twice you will disown me three times." And he broke down and wept.

● Cite an example from your life in which you denied the existence of a relationship in

order to avoid the consequences. _____

_____

_____

◆ ◆ ◆

Denial has many faces and can be easily masked. It appears in different ways and operates in various fashions. Some recognizable forms are:

■ **Simple Denial:** Pretending that something does not exist when it really does (e.g., discounting physical symptoms that may indicate the presence of problems).

■ **Minimizing:** Being willing to acknowledge a problem, but unwilling to see its severity (e.g., admitting to estrangement in a relationship when in fact there is overt infidelity).

■ **Blaming:** Blame on someone else for causing the problem; the behavior is not denied, but its cause is someone else's fault (e.g., blaming your parents for your current inappropriate behavior).

■ **Excusing:** Offering excuses, alibis, justifications and other explanations for our own or others' behavior (e.g., calling in sick for a partner when the actual cause of the absence is drunkenness).

■ **Generalizing:** Dealing with problems on a general level, but avoiding personal and emotional awareness of the situation or conditions (e.g., sympathizing with a friend's flu symptoms when you know chemical dependency is the underlying cause of the problem).

■ **Dodging:** Changing the subject to avoid threatening topics (e.g., becoming adept at "small talk").

■ **Attacking:** Becoming angry and irritable when reference is made to the existing condition, thus avoiding the issue (e.g., being unwilling to share your feelings).

- When and how is denial most active in your life? _____
  _____
  _____
  _____

GALATIANS 6:3-5

If anyone thinks he is something when he is nothing, he deceives himself. Each one should test his own actions. Then he can take pride in himself, without comparing himself to somebody else, for each one should carry his own load.

- How does pride interfere with your ability to be honest with yourself? _____
  _____
  _____
  _____

◆ ◆ ◆

Taking a personal inventory is similar to cleaning a closet. We take stock of what we have, examine what we want to save and discard what is no longer useful or appropriate. It doesn't have to be done all at once, but it will have to be done eventually. If we take small sections at a time, the cleaning is more thorough and the long-term results are better. In the same way that clothes can trigger memories of the past, our inventory may provoke both good and bad memories. We must remember that the past is only history. It is not the purpose of our inventory to dwell on the past. This reflection is only a tool to help us understand our current behavior patterns. Our main concern now is for our future. Approaching the inventory in this manner can lessen our fears surrounding this task.

- What anxieties do you have about memories of your past? _____
  _____
  _____
  _____

LAMENTATIONS 3:40

Let us examine our ways and test them, and let us return to the Lord.

- How will examining your ways help you return to the Lord? _____
  _____
  _____
  _____

◆ ◆ ◆

In Step Four, we will get in touch with many of the behaviors and attitudes that have been with us since childhood. Our emerging awareness about the way we were raised will help us understand that our present behaviors are natural outgrowths of our early need to survive. As adults, we are now in a position to choose a different lifestyle for ourselves. We can learn to conduct ourselves in a manner that is nurturing to us. As we look at our strengths and weaknesses, we will become aware of the areas of our lives that need to be strengthened. We will also see those areas in which we exhibit strength through our wise choices. We can use the inventory to decide which areas of our lives need changing, and which areas seem to be the way we want them to be.

- Which of your present behaviors is the most damaging to your life? Explain. _____

_____

_____

_____

PSALM 139:23-24

Search me, O God, and know my heart; test me and know my anxious thoughts. See if there is any offensive way in me, and lead me in the way everlasting.

- How can asking God to search you and know your heart help you see your faults and lead

  you to a better life? _____

_____

_____

_____

◆ ◆ ◆

Our next task is to look at resentment and recognize how damaging it is to us. It is the "number-one" offender and often the major cause of spiritual disease. As we list our resentments, we see how they have affected our self-esteem, our well-being and our personal relationships. Holding on to resentment causes stress, anxiety and uncontrollable feelings of anger. If these are unresolved, serious emotional and physical consequences will develop. If we allow our resentments to prevail, serious depression can develop and ultimately destroy us.

- List your major resentment. How is it interfering with your life? _____

_____

_____

_____

JAMES 1:19-21

My dear brothers, take note of this: Everyone should be quick to listen, slow to speak and slow to become angry, for man's anger does not bring about the righteous life that God desires. Therefore, get rid of all moral filth and the evil that is so prevalent, and humbly accept the word planted in you, which can save you.

- List situations where you became angry as a result of your resentments. _____

_____

_____

_____

◆ ◆ ◆

The second most destructive offender is fear. It is the emotion we most strongly feel when we begin to look at ourselves. When fear is present, our need to deny, ignore and avoid reality is increased. Our unrealistic perspective becomes greatly exaggerated and intensifies our emotional responses. Fear can cause us a great deal of pain. It attacks us physically and causes feelings that range from apprehension to panic. When fear is present, we may become nervous, nauseated or disoriented. As we inventory our fears, we may discover that they are a direct result of our inability to make decisions. Or we may believe that, if we could make the *right* decisions, things would be different.

● List your major fear. How is it interfering with your life? _____
_____
_____
_____

1 JOHN 4:18
There is no fear in love. But perfect love drives out fear, because fear has to do with punishment. The man who fears is not made perfect in love.

● What fears surface when you realize God knows all your faults? _____
_____
_____
_____

◆ ◆ ◆

Facing our resentments and fears requires a great deal of courage. Our past tendency has been to shut down our feelings. Now we begin to look at areas of our lives that we have never seen before. It is important to realize that God is with us and will help us every step of our way. As Christians, we have the added support of knowing that the Lord understands and shares our struggle. With God's help and understanding, the pain will diminish.

● How does being a Christian give you added support in dealing with your resentments and fears? _____
_____
_____
_____

2 CORINTHIANS 13:5-6
Examine yourselves to see whether you are in the faith; test yourselves. Do you not realize that Christ Jesus is in you—unless, of course, you fail the test? And I trust that you will discover that we have not failed the test.

● Cite situations that show you are in the faith and Christ is in you. _____
_____
_____
_____

● ● ●

As part of the Step Four inventory, we will look at our character traits and see our strengths and weaknesses. Our strengths appear in behavior that has positive effects on us as well as on others. Our weaknesses are manifested in behavior that is destructive to ourselves and others. Before we can correct our problem areas, we need to acknowledge and examine both. Understanding begins when we discover how we became the people we are—how we formulated the ideas, beliefs and attitudes that govern how we act.

● What is your major strength? How does it support you? _____

_____

_____

_____

● What is your major weakness? How does it hurt you? _____

_____

_____

_____

EPHESIANS 4:31
Get rid of all bitterness, rage and anger, brawling and slander, along with every form of malice.

● How does Step Four help you identify your bitterness, rage and other forms of malice?

_____

_____

_____

_____

◆ ◆ ◆

When preparing your inventory, you may encounter some difficulties. If you appear to be blocked at some point, denial may be operating. Stop for a moment and reflect on what you are attempting to do. Take time to analyze your feelings. Ask God for help. In times like this, God's presence means a great deal to us, and we must be willing to look to God for support.

● What is your resistance to making your inventory? Explain. _____

_____

_____

_____

LAMENTATIONS 3:19-22
I remember my affliction and my wandering, the bitterness and the gall. I well remember them, and my soul is downcast within me. Yet this I call to mind and therefore I have hope: Because of the Lord's great love we are not consumed, for his compassions never fail.

● How does remembering your afflictions cause you to feel downcast? _____

_____

_____

_____

JAMES 1:12

Blessed is the man who perseveres under trial, because when he has stood the test, he will receive the crown of life that God has promised to those who love him.

● How are you able to recognize and appreciate the courage you must have to achieve the new life that God has for you? _____

_____

_____

_____

♦ ♦ ♦

The inventory we are preparing is for our own benefit. It will help us make a major breakthrough in our self-acceptance and lead us further along the road to recovery. As we proceed to Steps Five, Six and Seven, we will see the process continue to unfold. We will acknowledge the truth about ourselves, discuss it with others and, finally, ask God to remove our shortcomings.

● What is your main goal in preparing your inventory? _____

_____

_____

_____

COLOSSIANS 3:5-8

Put to death, therefore, whatever belongs to your earthly nature: sexual immorality, impurity, lust, evil desires and greed, which is idolatry. Because of these, the wrath of God is coming. You used to walk in these ways, in the life you once lived. But now you must rid yourselves of all such things as these: anger, rage, malice, slander, and filthy language from your lips.

● How has making your personal inventory helped you to seek healing? _____

_____

_____

_____

♦ ♦ ♦

IMPORTANT GUIDELINES IN PREPARING YOUR INVENTORY

The material offered in this Step Four Inventory Guide is somewhat different from the inventory guides used in other Twelve Step Programs. Emphasis is on those feelings and behaviors most commonly seen in Adult Children from homes where alcohol-related or other damage-inducing behavior was prevalent. When preparing your inventory, choose the traits that specifically apply to you. Don't tackle them all at once. Use recent events and record words and actions as accurately as possible. Take your time. It's better to be thorough with some than incomplete with all.

The inventory begins with exercises on resentments and fears, followed by a series of feelings and behaviors to be examined. This process enables you to prepare yourself for Step Five. You are the primary beneficiary of your honesty and thoroughness in this inventory.

It is important to refrain from generalizing. As you will note in the example provided for "Isolation," being specific helps identify active traits. When you list specific examples, include who, when, where, what. To the best of your ability, give the names of all persons involved in the situation with you (who); record the date the behavior took place (when); indicate where this behavior occurred (where); and, finally, describe the feeling or behavior.

RESENTMENT EXERCISE

Resentment is an underlying cause of many forms of spiritual disease. Our mental and physical ills are frequently the direct result of this unhealthy condition. Learning to deal with resentment in a healthy way is an important part of our recovery process.

List situations in which resentment is a problem for you. Answer the following questions when describing these conditions:

- What or whom do you resent (e.g., people, institutions, principles)?

- Why are you resentful (e.g., what happened to cause this resentment)?

- How has this resentment affected you (e.g., lowered self-esteem, loss of employment, difficulty in relationships, physical harm or threats)?

- Which character defect is active (e.g., approval seeking, control, fear of abandonment)?

EXAMPLE: **I resent** my boss **because** he doesn't care to hear my explanation of why I am depressed. **This affects** my self-esteem. **This activates** unexpressed anger.

- I resent _____

  Because _____

  This affects _____

  This activates _____

- I resent _____

  Because _____

  This affects _____

  This activates _____

- I resent _____

  Because _____

  This affects _____

  This activates _____

- I resent _____

  Because _____

  This affects _____

  This activates _____

- I resent _____

  Because _____

  This affects _____

  This activates _____

FEAR EXERCISE

Fear is an underlying cause of many forms of spiritual disease. A wide range of mental and physical ills are frequently the direct result of this unwholesome condition. Learning to acknowledge fear in a healthy way is an important part of our recovery process.

List situations in which fear is a problem for you. Answer the following questions when describing these conditions:

- What or whom do you fear (e.g., people, institutions, principles)?
- Why are you fearful (e.g., what happened to cause this fear)?
- How has this fear affected you (e.g., lowered self-esteem, difficulty in relationships, diminished goals, procrastination)?
- Which character defect is active (e.g., approval seeking, control, fear of abandonment)?

EXAMPLE: **I fear** my spouse **because** I feel that I am never able to please him/her. **This affects** my self-esteem and sexuality. **This activates** my fear of abandonment.

- I fear _____

  Because _____

  This affects _____

  This activates _____

- I fear _____

  Because _____

  This affects _____

  This activates _____

- I fear _____

  Because _____

  This affects _____

  This activates _____

- I fear _____

  Because _____

  This affects _____

  This activates _____

- I fear _____

  Because _____

  This affects _____

  This activates _____

CHARACTER TRAITS (WEAKNESSES)

The example below will assist you in completing the questions asked as part of your Fourth Step Inventory. Follow the suggested guidelines and be as thorough as possible. Refer to **Isolation** on page 60 for definitions.

ISOLATION

● List specific examples of your behavior that indicate you are isolating yourself; e.g.,

I declined an invitation to Sharon's party last Saturday, because I feared I would be unable to participate.

I felt embarrassed at work when my supervisor asked me why I did not actively participate in the management meeting.

_____

_____

_____

_____

_____

● Identify and explain the underlying causes (such as fear, resentment, anger, guilt); e.g.,

I am afraid that if I let myself go I will do something foolish. This inhibits my ability to have fun. I worry about not fitting in or being conspicuous.

I fear personal criticism if I express myself freely. Instead, I isolate myself by not talking.

_____

_____

_____

_____

_____

● Identify and explain what is being hurt and threatened (such as self-esteem, goals, security, personal or sexual relations); e.g.,

My self-esteem is affected when I reveal myself to other people. I judge myself without mercy. This interferes with my desire to have a love relationship and to meet new people.

I feel my job security is at risk.

_____

_____

_____

_____

_____

CHARACTER TRAITS (STRENGTHS)

The example below will assist you in completing the questions asked as part of your Fourth Step Inventory. Follow the suggested guidelines and be as thorough as possible. Refer to **Recovery from Isolation** on page 61 for definitions.

RECOVERY FROM ISOLATION

- List specific examples of your behavior that indicate you isolate less frequently than before; e.g.,

Today I went to lunch with Diane and Evelyn. I felt comfortable and at ease, and was able to share in the conversation. I risked sharing some special feelings about my desire to be in an intimate relationship. I did not feel threatened, because I could see that they were seriously listening and would respect my confidentiality.

During last Monday's management meeting, I expressed a concern relative to risking business expenses. Rather than being criticized, I was thanked for taking the time to provide the insight.

_____

_____

_____

_____

_____

_____

_____

_____

_____

- What do you hope to achieve as you become more confident about situations in which you would usually isolate yourself; e.g.,

I want to cultivate new, healthy relationships that will expand my confidence and help me be more comfortable in social settings. I hope to become more flexible so that I can learn to be spontaneous and have fun.

I want to become more assertive and participatory in business settings. I believe this will give me an opportunity to realize my full potential.

_____

_____

_____

_____

_____

_____

_____

_____

REPRESSED ANGER

Anger is a major source of many problems in the lives of Adult Children. It is a feeling that we often suppress, because admitting it makes us uncomfortable. In our chaotic homes, the turmoil was so intense that we either denied our anger or expressed it inappropriately. We felt it was safer to protect ourselves and simply hoped our feelings would go away. We were not aware that repressed anger can lead to serious resentment and depression. It causes physical complications that can lead to stress-related illnesses. Denying anger or expressing it inappropriately causes problems in relationships, because we cannot be truthful about our feelings and must always be pretending.

When we repress anger, we may experience:

Resentment	**Depression**
Self-Pity	**Sadness**
Jealousy	**Stress**
Anxiety	**Physical discomfort**

- List specific examples of your behavior that indicate you are angry. _____

_____

_____

_____

_____

_____

_____

- Identify and explain the underlying causes of your difficulty in dealing with anger. ____

_____

_____

_____

_____

_____

_____

- Identify and explain what you feel is being hurt and threatened by your feelings of anger. _____

_____

_____

_____

_____

_____

_____

RECOVERY FROM REPRESSED ANGER

Learning to express anger is a major step in our recovery. It releases many hidden emotions and allows healing to take place. Expressing anger lets others know our limits and helps us to be honest with ourselves. As we learn to express anger more appropriately, we are better able to cope with our own hostility as well as the anger of others. Our relationships improve as we begin to feel comfortable expressing ourselves. Stress-related problems diminish, and we even feel better physically.

As we recover from repressed anger, we begin to:

Express anger   **Set limits for ourselves**
Identify hurt feelings   **Enjoy inner peace**
Make reasonable requests   **Reduce stress and anxiety**

● List specific examples of your behavior that indicate you can express anger in a healthy way. _____

_____

_____

_____

_____

_____

_____

_____

_____

_____

● What do you hope to achieve as you identify and release your anger? _____

_____

_____

_____

_____

_____

_____

_____

_____

_____

APPROVAL SEEKING

As a result of our dysfunctional upbringing, we fear disapproval and criticism. As children, we desperately wanted to receive approval from our parents, grandparents, siblings and significant others. This rarely occurred for most of us. As a result we were constantly seeking validation of ourselves. This need for approval continued into adulthood and seriously affected the way we pattern our lives and thinking around the needs of others. Rather than look for approval in a positive way, we seek validation in order to feel better about ourselves, and get people to like us. This keeps us out of touch with our own feelings and desires, and prevents us from discovering our own wants and needs. We look for reactions in others, and attempt to manage their impression of us. We constantly strive to please everyone and often stay in relationships that are destructive to us.

When we have a need for approval from others, we may be:

People pleasing	**Feeling unworthy**
Fearing criticism	**Ignoring our own needs**
Fearing failure	**Lacking in confidence**

- List specific examples of your behavior that indicate you seek approval from others.

  _____

  _____

  _____

  _____

  _____

  _____

  _____

- Identify and explain the underlying causes of your approval seeking. _____

  _____

  _____

  _____

  _____

  _____

  _____

- Identify and explain what you feel is being hurt and threatened by your need for

  approval? _____

  _____

  _____

  _____

  _____

  _____

  _____

RECOVERY FROM APPROVAL SEEKING

As we begin to rely on our own approval and that of our Higher Power, we understand that wanting approval is okay, and we learn to ask for it rather than manipulate others to get it. We accept compliments from others and learn to simply say "thank you," believing that the compliment is sincere. We say yes when it is a comfortable answer. We are willing to say "no" when "no" is appropriate.

As we recover from inappropriate approval seeking, we begin to:

Recognize our own needs   **Be loyal to oneself**
Tell the truth about how we feel **Build our confidence**

- List specific examples of your behavior that indicate you are not seeking approval only from other people. _____

_____

_____

_____

_____

_____

_____

_____

_____

_____

_____

_____

- What do you hope to achieve as your need for outside approval lessens? _____

_____

_____

_____

_____

_____

_____

_____

_____

_____

_____

_____

_____

CARETAKING

As long as we took care of others, solved their problems, and supplied their needs, we did not have time to look at ourselves. As this trait became more pronounced, we completely lost our own identity. As children, we assumed the responsibility for concerns and problems of others that were far beyond our capability to handle, and as a result, were deprived of a normal childhood. The unrealistic demands placed on us, and the praise we received for being "little adults," made us believe we had God-like powers. Taking care of others boosted our self-esteem and made us feel indispensable. It gave purpose to our lives. As caretakers, we are most comfortable with chaotic situations in which we are often assured that we are needed. Although we often resent others for taking and not giving, we are unable to allow others to care for us. We don't allow ourselves the joy of taking care of ourselves.

As caretakers, we may:

Make ourselves indispensable	**Lose our identity**
Rescue people	**Feel super-responsible**
Ignore our own needs	**Become co-dependent**

- List specific examples of your behavior that indicate you are acting as a caretaker. _____
  _____
  _____
  _____
  _____
  _____
  _____

- Identify and explain the underlying causes of your need to take care of others. _____
  _____
  _____
  _____
  _____
  _____
  _____

- Identify and explain what you feel is being hurt and threatened by your role as a caretaker. _____
  _____
  _____
  _____
  _____
  _____
  _____

RECOVERY FROM CARETAKING

As we put aside the role of caretaker, we become less and less responsible for everyone and everything and allow individuals to find their own way. We give them over to the care of their Higher Power, which is the best source for their guidance, love and support. By dropping the burden of meeting everyone's needs, we find time to develop our own personalities. Our obsession with caring for others is replaced by an acceptance of the fact that ultimately we have no power over the lives of others. We realize that our main responsibility in life is for our own welfare and happiness, and we turn other people over to God's care.

When we stop being caretakers, we begin to:

Stop rescuing others　　　　　　　　**Develop our own identity**
Take care of ourselves　　　　　　　**Recognize dependent relationships**
Set limits

● List specific examples of your behavior that indicate you are no longer being a caretaker.

_____

_____

_____

_____

_____

_____

_____

_____

_____

_____

● What do you hope to achieve as you become more aware of your needs and stop being a caretaker? _____

_____

_____

_____

_____

_____

_____

_____

_____

CONTROL

As children, we had little or no control over our environment or the events that took place in our lives. As adults, we have extraordinary needs to control our feelings and behavior and we try to control the feelings and behavior of others. We become rigid and unable to have spontaneity in our lives. We trust only ourselves to complete a task or to handle a situation. We manipulate others in order to gain their approval, and keep a balance of control that makes us feel safe. We fear that our lives will deteriorate if we give up our management position. We become stressed and anxious when our authority is threatened.

Due to our need to be in control, we may:

Overreact to change	**Be judgmental and rigid**
Lack trust	**Be intolerant**
Fear failure	**Manipulate others**

- List specific examples of your behavior that indicate you are attempting to control or manipulate people or situations. _____

_____

_____

_____

_____

_____

_____

- Identify and explain the underlying causes of your need to be in control. _____

_____

_____

_____

_____

_____

_____

- Identify and explain what you feel is being hurt and threatened by your need for control? _____

_____

_____

_____

_____

_____

_____

RECOVERY FROM CONTROL

As we become more aware of the way we have attempted to control people and things, we begin to realize that our efforts have in fact been useless—that we did not control anything or anyone except ourselves. We discover more effective ways to get our needs met when we start accepting God as the source of our security. As we begin to surrender our wills and our lives to His care, we will experience less stress and anxiety. We become more able to participate in activities without being primarily concerned with the outcome. Saying the Serenity Prayer is helpful whenever we begin to recognize the reappearance of our need for control.

As we learn to give up control, we begin to:

Accept change	**Reduce our stress levels**
Trust in ourselves	**Find ways to have fun**
Empower others	**Accept others as they are**

● List specific examples of your behavior that indicate you no longer feel a need to be in control. _____

_____

_____

_____

_____

_____

_____

_____

_____

_____

_____

_____

● What do you hope to achieve as you become less controlling? _____

_____

_____

_____

_____

_____

_____

_____

_____

_____

_____

_____

FEAR OF ABANDONMENT

Fear of abandonment is a reaction to stress that we developed in early childhood. As children, we observed unpredictable behavior from responsible adults. Never knowing from one day to the next whether or not our parents would be there for us, many of us were abandoned either physically or emotionally. As their addiction increased in severity, so did their inability to parent. As children we simply did not exist. As adults, we are inclined to choose partners with whom we can repeat this fear. We try to be perfect by meeting all our partner's needs in order to avoid experiencing the pain of abandonment. Reducing the possibility of abandonment takes precedence over dealing with issues or conflicts and produces a tense environment with poor communication.

When we fear abandonment, we may:

Feel insecure	**Worry excessively**
Be caretakers	**Feel guilty when standing up for ourselves**
Avoid being alone	**Become co-dependent**

- List specific examples of your behavior that indicate you fear abandonment. _____
_____
_____
_____
_____
_____
_____

- Identify and explain the underlying causes of your fear of abandonment. _____
_____
_____
_____
_____
_____
_____

- Identify and explain what you feel is being hurt and threatened by your fear of being abandoned. _____
_____
_____
_____
_____
_____
_____

RECOVERY FROM FEAR OF ABANDONMENT

As we learn to rely more upon the ever-present love of God, our confidence in our ability to manage our environment increases. Our fear of abandonment diminishes and is replaced by the feeling that we are worthy people in our own right. We seek out healthy relationships with people who love and take care of themselves. We feel more secure in revealing our feelings. We transfer our old dependence on others to trust in God. We learn to understand and accept a nurturing and loving fellowship within our community. Our self-confidence grows as we begin to realize that with God in our lives, we will never again be totally alone.

As fear of abandonment diminishes, we begin to:

Be honest about our feelings   **Consider our own needs in a relationship**
Feel comfortable being alone   **Reduce our caretaking and**
Express confidence   **co-dependency traits**

- List specific examples of your behavior that indicate you no longer fear abandonment.

_____
_____
_____
_____
_____
_____
_____
_____
_____
_____
_____

- What goals do you hope to achieve as your fear of abandonment lessens? _____

_____
_____
_____
_____
_____
_____
_____
_____
_____
_____
_____
_____

FEAR OF AUTHORITY FIGURES

Fear of people in roles of authority can be a result of our parents' unrealistic expectations of us—wanting us to be more than we were able to be. We see people in authority as having unrealistic expectations of us and fear we cannot meet their expectations. We are unable to deal with people whom we perceive as being in positions of power. Simple assertiveness displayed by others is often misinterpreted by us as anger. This can cause us to feel intimidated and to become oversensitive. No matter how competent we are, we compare ourselves to others and conclude that we are inadequate. As a result, we constantly compromise our integrity in order to avoid confrontation or criticism.

Fear of authority figures may cause us to:

Fear rejection	**Compare ourselves to others**
Take things personally	**React rather than act**
Be arrogant to cover up	**Feel inadequate**

- List specific examples of your behavior that indicate you fear people in roles of authority.

_____

_____

_____

_____

_____

_____

- Identify and explain the underlying causes of your fear. _____

_____

_____

_____

_____

_____

_____

- Identify and explain what you feel is being hurt and threatened by your fear of authority figures. _____

_____

_____

_____

_____

_____

_____

RECOVERY FROM FEAR OF AUTHORITY FIGURES

As we begin to feel comfortable with people in roles of authority, we learn to put our focus on ourselves and discover that we have nothing to fear. We recognize others as being like us, with their own fears, defenses and insecurities. Others' behavior no longer dictates how we feel about ourselves. We start acting rather than reacting when responding to others. We recognize that our ultimate authority figure is God and that He is always with us.

As we become comfortable with authority figures, we begin to:

Act with increased self-esteem   **Accept constructive criticism**
Stand up for ourselves   **Interact easily with people in authority**

- List specific examples of your behavior that indicate you are gaining confidence around people in authority. _____

_____

_____

_____

_____

_____

_____

_____

_____

_____

- What do you hope to achieve as you become more confident and secure around people in authority? _____

_____

_____

_____

_____

_____

_____

_____

_____

_____

_____

FROZEN FEELINGS

Many of us have difficulty expressing our feelings or even realizing that we have them. We harbor deep emotional pain and a sense of guilt and shame. As children, our feelings were met with disapproval, anger and rejection. As a means of survival, we learned to hide our feelings or repress them entirely. As adults, we are not in touch with our feelings. We can only allow ourselves to have "acceptable" feelings in order to stay "safe." Our true nature is distorted in order to protect ourselves from the reality of what is actually happening. Distorted and repressed feelings cause resentment, anger, and depression, which often leads to physical illness.

When we have frozen feelings, we may:

Be unaware of our feelings　　　**Experience depression**
Have distorted feelings　　　　**Develop physical illness**
Suppress our feelings

- List specific examples of your behavior that indicate you are not expressing your feelings.

_____

_____

_____

_____

_____

_____

_____

- Identify and explain the underlying causes of your inability to express your feelings. __

_____

_____

_____

_____

_____

_____

- Identify and explain what is being hurt and threatened by not expressing your feelings. __

_____

_____

_____

_____

_____

_____

RECOVERY FROM FROZEN FEELINGS

As we get in touch with our feelings and learn to express them, strange things begin to happen. Our stress levels decrease as we become able to express ourselves honestly, and we begin to see ourselves as worthy. We learn that expression of true feelings is the healthy way to communicate, and we find that more of our own needs are being met. All we have to do is ask. As we begin to release our feelings, we experience some levels of pain. But, as our courage increases the pain goes away, and we develop a sense of peace and serenity. The more willing we are to take risks in releasing our emotions, the more effective our recovery will be.

As we experience and express our feelings, we begin to:

Feel free to cry	**Experience our true self**
Openly express feelings	**Express our needs to others**

- List specific examples of your behavior that indicate you are becoming aware of your feelings and are able to express them. _____

_____

_____

_____

_____

_____

_____

_____

_____

_____

_____

- What do you hope to achieve as you become more comfortable with expressing your feelings? _____

_____

_____

_____

_____

_____

_____

_____

_____

_____

_____

ISOLATION

We find it safe in many instances to withdraw from surroundings that are uncomfortable for us. By isolating ourselves, we prevent others from seeing us as we really are. We tell ourselves that we are not worthy and, therefore, do not deserve love, attention or acceptance. We also tell ourselves that we cannot be punished or hurt if we don't express our feelings. Rather than take risks, we choose to hide, thereby eliminating the need to face an uncertain outcome.

When we isolate ourselves, we may be:

Fearing rejection	**Feeling defeated**
Experiencing loneliness	**Non-assertive**
Procrastinating	**Seeing ourselves as different from others**

● List specific examples of your behavior that indicate you are isolating yourself. _____

_____

_____

_____

_____

_____

_____

_____

● Identify and explain the underlying causes of your desire to isolate. _____

_____

_____

_____

_____

_____

_____

_____

● Identify and explain what you feel is being hurt and threatened by your isolation. _____

_____

_____

_____

_____

_____

_____

_____

RECOVERY FROM ISOLATION

As we begin to feel better about ourselves, we become more willing to take risks and expose ourselves to new surroundings. We seek friends and relationships that are nurturing, safe, and supportive. We learn to participate and to have fun in group activities. It becomes easier to express our feelings as we develop a stronger sense of self-esteem. We recognize that people will accept us for who we really are. Our self-acceptance allows us to experience the precious gift of living more comfortably and serenely.

As we isolate less often, we begin to:

Accept ourselves　　　　　　　　**Complete projects**
Freely express our emotions　　**Actively participate with others**
Cultivate supportive relationships

● List specific examples of your behavior that indicate you isolate yourself less frequently.

_____

_____

_____

_____

_____

_____

_____

_____

_____

_____

_____

● What do you hope to achieve as you feel more confident about situations from which you would usually isolate yourself? _____

_____

_____

_____

_____

_____

_____

_____

_____

_____

LOW SELF-ESTEEM

Low self-esteem is rooted in our early childhood, during which we were never encouraged to believe that we were adequate. As a result of constant criticism, we believed that we were "bad" and the cause of many family problems. To feel accepted, we tried harder to please. The harder we tried, the more frustrated we became. Low self-esteem affects our ability to set and achieve goals. We are afraid to take risks. We feel responsible for things that go wrong, and when something goes right, we do not give ourselves credit. Instead, we feel undeserving and believe it is not going to last.

When we experience low self-esteem, we may:

Be non-assertive	**Isolate from others**
Fear failure	**Have a negative self-image**
Appear inadequate	**Need to be perfect**
Fear rejection	

● List specific examples of your behavior that indicate you have low self-esteem. _____

_____

_____

_____

_____

_____

_____

● Identify and explain the underlying causes of your low self-esteem. _____

_____

_____

_____

_____

_____

_____

● Identify and explain what you feel is being hurt and threatened by your low self-esteem.

_____

_____

_____

_____

_____

_____

_____

RECOVERY FROM LOW SELF-ESTEEM

As we work with our Higher Power to build confidence in ourselves and our abilities, our self-esteem increases. We are able to interact with others and to accept ourselves as we really are. We see our strengths as well as our limitations and learn to accept ourselves at face value. We become more willing to take risks; we realize we can achieve many things that we had never dreamed would be possible. Sharing feelings with others becomes more comfortable— we feel safer as we come to know others and allow them to know us. Relationships become healthier, because we are able to trust and validate ourselves, and no longer need to look to others for validation.

As our self-esteem increases, we begin to:

Be more confident   **Love ourselves**
Act more assertively   **Openly express feelings**
Easily interact with others   **Take risks**

- List specific examples of your behavior that indicate your self-esteem is improving. ____

_____

_____

_____

_____

_____

_____

_____

_____

_____

_____

- What do you hope to achieve as you feel better about yourself? _____

_____

_____

_____

_____

_____

_____

_____

_____

_____

_____

_____

OVERDEVELOPED SENSE OF RESPONSIBILITY

As children in a dysfunctional home, we felt responsible for our parents' problems. We tried to be "model children" and make things be the way we thought others wanted them to be. We believed that we were responsible for the emotions and actions of others; even for the outcome of events. Today we remain supersensitive to the needs of others, and we try to assume responsibility for helping them get their needs met. It is important to us to be perfect. We volunteer to do things so people will appreciate us. Our sense of responsibility causes us to over-commit, and we have a tendency to take on more than we are capable of handling effectively.

When we are overly responsible, we may:

Take life too seriously	**Be a high achiever**
Appear rigid	**Have false pride**
Be perfectionists	**Manipulate others**
Assume responsibility for others	

- List specific examples of your behavior that indicate you are being overly responsible.

_____

_____

_____

_____

_____

_____

_____

- Identify and explain the underlying causes for your being overly responsible. _____

_____

_____

_____

_____

_____

_____

- Identify and explain what you feel is being hurt and threatened when you are overly responsible. _____

_____

_____

_____

_____

_____

_____

RECOVERY FROM OVERDEVELOPED SENSE OF RESPONSIBILITY

Accepting the fact that we are not responsible for the actions and feelings of others forces us to focus on ourselves. We understand that we do not influence the lives of others and that people are responsible for themselves. As we assume responsibility for our own actions, we become aware that we must rely on God for guidance and take care of our own needs. Then we will find time and energy to support and nurture ourselves.

As we stop being overly responsible, we begin to:

Take care of ourselves   **Accept our limitations**
Enjoy leisure time   **Delegate responsibility**

- List specific examples of your behavior that indicate you are not taking responsibility for others. _____

_____

_____

_____

_____

_____

_____

_____

_____

_____

- What do you hope to achieve as you allow others to take responsibility for themselves and begin taking care of yourself? _____

_____

_____

_____

_____

_____

_____

_____

_____

_____

_____

REPRESSED SEXUALITY

We find ourselves confused and uncertain about our sexual feelings toward others, particularly those to whom we are close or those with whom we hope to be emotionally intimate. We have been trained to think of our sexual feelings as unnatural or abnormal. Because we do not share our feelings with others, we have no opportunity to develop a healthy attitude about our own sexuality. As small children, we may have explored our physical sexuality with peers and been severely punished. The message was "sex is dirty, is not talked about, and is to be avoided." Some of us saw our parents as very disapproving or even as totally nonsexual beings. We may have been molested by a parent or close relative who was out of control. As a result, we are uncomfortable in our sexual roles. We do not freely discuss sex with our partners for fear of being misunderstood and abandoned. As parents, we may avoid discussing sexuality with our children and deny their need for developing a sexual identity.

Due to repressed sexuality we may:

Feel guilt and shame
Lose our sense of morality
Be confused about our sexual identity
Be lustful

Be incest victims
Experience being frigid or impotent
Manipulate others by seductive behavior

- List specific examples of your behavior that indicate you have problems dealing with your sexuality. _____

_____

_____

_____

_____

_____

- Identify and explain the underlying causes of confusion about your sexuality. _____

_____

_____

_____

_____

- Identify and explain what you feel is being hurt and threatened by your inability to express your sexual feelings. _____

_____

_____

_____

_____

_____

RECOVERY FROM REPRESSED SEXUALITY

Relying upon the constant love of our Lord, our self-worth increases and we see ourselves as worthy in His eyes and in the eyes of others. As we increase our self-love and our ability to take care of ourselves, we seek to be with other healthy people who love and take care of themselves. We are less fearful of commitment and are better prepared to enter into a healthy relationship—emotionally, intellectually, and sexually. We feel more secure in sharing our feelings, strengths, and weaknesses. Our self-confidence grows and allows us to be vulnerable. We give up the need for perfection in ourselves and others and, in so doing, open ourselves to growth and change. We are honest about our own sexuality with our children. We accept their need for information as well as their need for a healthy sexual identity.

When we accept our sexuality, we begin to:

Communicate openly about sex **Consider our own sexual needs**
Accept our sexual self **Share intimate feelings**

- List specific examples of how your behavior is improving. _____

_____

_____

_____

_____

_____

_____

_____

_____

_____

_____

- What do you hope to achieve as you feel more confident with your sexuality? _____

_____

_____

_____

_____

_____

_____

_____

_____

_____

_____

_____

67

Notes: _____

STEP FIVE

Admitted to God, to ourselves, and to another human being the exact nature of our wrongs.

Therefore confess your sins to each other and pray for each other so that you may be healed.
(James 5:16a)

Step Four laid the foundation for identifying many of our shadowy deeds and thoughts, as well as for recording the strengths we have developed from childhood patterns of survival. Completing our Step Four inventory has made us aware of many truths about ourselves. This realization may have caused us pain. The natural reaction is to feel sadness or guilt or both. We have faced ourselves and our history honestly. We have courageously identified some behaviors we want to eliminate and others we want to develop in the future.

For those of us who have been honest and thorough, Step Four has provided the foundation upon which we will build our recovery. It identified the unresolved feelings, unhealed memories and personal defects that have produced resentment, depression and loss of self-worth. Asking God for help and acknowledging that God is light (John 1:5-9) helped us commit our lives to walking in the light of His truth. Acknowledging our wrongs and moving toward restoration of our self-worth lifted a great burden from our hearts and minds. Now that we have identified all of our character traits, it is possible to relieve ourselves of the burden of guilt and shame associated with our wrong-doings. This step requires that we engage in honest confrontations with ourselves and others, by admitting our faults to God, to ourselves, and to another person. By doing so, we begin the important phase of setting aside our pride so that we can see ourselves in true perspective.

Admitting the exact nature of our wrongs to God is the first phase of Step Five. Here, we confess to God all that we have worked so hard to conceal. It is no longer necessary to blame God or others for what has happened to us, but rather to accept our history for exactly what it is. This brings us closer to God, and we begin to know that He is always there for us. Our confession helps us receive God's love and accept ourselves unconditionally. We must remember that we are all children of God and will never be rejected.

Admitting our wrongs to ourselves began in Step Four, as we wrote our inventory and had the opportunity to see our behaviors for what they really are. In Step Five, as we consciously admit our wrongs, we develop the desire and strength to release them. This builds our self-esteem and supports us as we move toward Step Seven, where we ask God to remove our shortcomings.

Telling our story to another person can be a frightening experience. Many of us have spent a major portion of our lives building defenses to keep others out. Living in isolation has been a way of protecting ourselves from further hurt. Step Five is our pathway out of isolation and loneliness. It is a move toward wholeness, happiness and a sense of peace. It is a humbling experience, as we are required to be totally honest. We can no longer pretend; it is time to reveal ourselves completely.

We will unveil parts of our nature that we have concealed from ourselves. We may fear the impact that our truthfulness will have on our lives. Telling our story to another person may cause us the additional fear of being rejected. However, it is essential that we take this important risk and confess our wrongs. With God's help, we will have the courage to disclose our true natures. The result will be worth all the agony of the unburdening process.

Ask for God's help in choosing the person to whom you will confess. Remember that the other believer should reflect the image of Christ and be a spokesman for Him. God intended us to speak to others, to share our sorrows and joys as members of His family. Look for qualities you admire in the other person which will inspire your confidence. Find someone on an equal spiritual level, with similar understanding. God's Holy Spirit works spiritually through all of His children. Sharing our personal experiences will help us come to know the depth of God's unconditional love for all His human family.

Personal Reflection

As we prepare for Step Five, we see how our growing relationship with God has given us the courage to examine ourselves, accept who we are and reveal our true selves. Step Five helps us acknowledge and discard our old survival skills and move toward a new and healthier life. Being thorough and honest in completing our inventory places us in a position to face the facts and move forward.

● Describe some feelings you experienced when making your inventory. _____

_____

_____

_____

JAMES 4:7-8
Submit yourselves, then, to God. Resist the devil, and he will flee from you. Come near to God and He will come near to you. Wash your hands, you sinners, and purify your hearts, you double-minded.

● How did completing your inventory purify your heart and bring you closer to God? ____

_____

_____

_____

◆ ◆ ◆

Step Five consists of three distinct parts. We will confess our faults to God, to ourselves and to another human being. For some of us, it will involve telling our life story for the first time. As we do it, we will cleanse ourselves of the excess baggage we have been carrying. As we open our hearts and reveal ourselves, we will achieve a deeper level of spirituality.

● What are your expectations and fears surrounding Step Five? _____

_____

_____

_____

JEREMIAH 14:20
O LORD, we acknowledge our wickedness and the guilt of our fathers; we have indeed sinned against you.

● Which of your faults is the most difficult to acknowledge? Why? _____

_____

_____

_____

◆ ◆ ◆

Admitting our defects to God can be very frightening. If we believe that God is in charge of the universe, that all events are His will, then blaming God can be a way for us to deny our part in the problem. It is important to understand that God has given us free will. He wants what is best for us, but He allows us to make choices free of His manipulation. As we admit our wrongs to Him, we see that His love for us is unconditional and everlasting. It becomes clear that He will strengthen and guide us, as we fulfill His desire for us to lead a healthy and peaceful life.

● Cite examples that illustrate God's unconditional love for you. _____

_____

_____

_____

ROMANS 14:12
So then, each of us will give an account of himself to God.

● Describe your experience of admitting your wrongs to God. _____

_____

_____

_____

◆ ◆ ◆

Our admission to ourselves is the least-threatening part of Step Five and can be done at minimal risk. Sharing our wrongs with ourselves doesn't force us to be honest, for we can easily deceive ourselves. Through denial, we have fooled ourselves all of our lives; confessing to ourselves only allows this pattern to continue. However, as a first step in getting to know our true selves, we must begin at this point.

● How does denial prevent you from being honest with yourself? _____

_____

_____

_____

1 JOHN 1:8-9
If we claim to be without sin, we deceive ourselves and the truth is not in us. If we confess our sins, he is faithful and just and will forgive us our sins and purify us from all unrighteousness.

● How will completing Step Five stop you from deceiving yourself? _____

_____

_____

_____

♦ ♦ ♦

Admitting our wrongs to another human being is the most powerful part of Step Five. It is a true exercise in humility and will help us begin the break down of our defenses. Being rigorously honest with another human being may be frightening enough to cause us to procrastinate in completing this portion of Step Five. It is tempting to believe that telling God is all that is necessary, because He ultimately forgives all sins. While this is true, it comes after our sharing with another person, for this is where our sense of self-worth begins.

● What do you expect to gain from admitting your faults to another person? _____

_____

_____

_____

● What is your resistance to sharing your story with another person? _____

_____

_____

_____

LUKE 15:17-19

> *"When he came to his senses, he said, 'How many of my father's hired men have food to spare, and here I am starving to death! I will set out and go back to my father and say to Him: Father, I have sinned against heaven and against you. I am no longer worthy to be called your son; make me like one of your hired men."*

● When confessing his sins, the Prodigal Son had to admit the terrible error of his ways.

Cite an example that illustrates your intent to do the same. _____

_____

_____

_____

♦ ♦ ♦

When choosing a person for Step Five, we will want to select a loving, caring person, one who will be there for us and who will provide unconditional acceptance. The person must be dependable, trustworthy and not be shocked or offended by what we reveal. It is wise to choose someone who is familiar with the Program. Sharing will flow easily if there is honesty and ample opportunity for feedback from the other person. Trusting the person with whom we share our story is vital to the success of Step Five and will provide a safe atmosphere.

● What qualities do you look for when choosing a person with whom to share your Fifth Step? _____

_____

_____

_____

PSALM 32:3-5

When I kept silent, my bones wasted away through my groaning all day long. For day and night your hand was heavy upon me; my strength was sapped as in the heat of summer...Then I acknowledged my sin to you and did not cover up my iniquity. I said, "I will confess my transgressions to the LORD"—and you forgave the guilt of my sin...

● How has carrying the burden of your wrongs caused you to groan and have no strength?

_____

_____

_____

◆ ◆ ◆

In telling our story to another person, we can expect more than just being heard. We must be ready to listen to the other person's response. The interchange can be helpful and productive if we are willing to listen with an open mind to the other person's viewpoint. This broadens our awareness of ourselves and gives us an opportunity to change and grow. Feedback is vital to us as a means of completing the process of revelation. Questions asked in a caring and understanding manner can reveal insights and feelings of which we are unaware. Sharing our life story in this way can be the most important interaction of our lives.

● How will feedback support you in completing your Fifth Step? _____

_____

_____

_____

● What can be gained by listening to the other person's viewpoint? _____

_____

_____

_____

JAMES 5:16

Therefore confess your sins to each other and pray for each other so that you may be healed. The prayer of a righteous man is powerful and effective.

● How is prayer helpful in the healing process? _____

_____

_____

_____

PROVERBS 28:13

He who conceals his sins does not prosper, but whoever confesses and renounces them finds mercy.

- As you complete Step Five, how will confessing your sins help you find mercy? _____
  _____
  _____
  _____

◆ ◆ ◆

When Step Five is completed, some expectations may remain unfulfilled. We need to understand that God's timing is not always our timing. God works in each one of us according to our own capacity to respond to Him. We are not to submit to our anxiety, but rather to trust God. The real test of our Step Five admission is our willingness to trust that God will strengthen and develop our capacity to change our lives.

- Describe your feelings after completing Step Five. Do you feel closer to God and your fellows? _____
  _____
  _____
  _____

- What difficulties did you have while sharing? _____
  _____
  _____
  _____

PROVERBS 30:32
  "If you have played the fool and exalted yourself, or if you have planned evil, clap your hand over your mouth!"

- How did Step Five help you to accept your past? _____
  _____
  _____
  _____

◆ ◆ ◆

Upon completion of Step Five, we will realize that we are not always in control. It is not easy to change our old behavior patterns all at once. Admitting the exact nature of our wrongs does not stop us from acting in our old ways. We can expect to have moments of weakness, yet be strong in knowing that our relationship with God can help us overcome them. If we sincerely desire to change our ways, God will give us the strength and courage that we require.

- In what ways did Step Five bring you closer to God and help you gain a better opinion of yourself? _____
  _____
  _____
  _____

ROMANS 3:23
For all have sinned and fall short of the glory of God.

● What do you plan to do when you act in your old ways? _____

_____

_____

_____

◆ ◆ ◆

Notes: _____

_____

_____

_____

_____

_____

_____

_____

_____

_____

_____

_____

_____

_____

_____

_____

_____

_____

_____

_____

_____

_____

_____

_____

IMPORTANT GUIDELINES FOR PREPARING YOUR FIFTH STEP

Choose your Fifth Step listener carefully; one who is familiar with Twelve Step Programs. The individual can be:

- A clergyman ordained by an established religion. Ministers of many faiths often receive such requests.

- A trusted friend (preferably of the same sex), a doctor or psychologist.

- A family member with whom you can openly share. Be careful not to disclose information that might be harmful to spouses or other family members.

- A member of a Twelve-Step Program. If you are working with family groups as described in this book, you may find trust already exists and will deepen by doing your Fifth Step with a group member. In some cases, the family group as a whole can be the listener.

In preparing for the Fifth Step, either as communicator or listener, the following suggestions are helpful:

- Begin with prayer, calling upon Christ Jesus to be present as you prepare to go through your Fourth Step revelations and insights. Ask God to guide and support you in what you are about to experience.

- Allow ample time to complete each thought and stay focused on the subject. Discourage unnecessary explanations.

- Eliminate distractions. Telephone calls, children, visitors and extraneous noises should be eliminated.

- Remember that Step Five asks only that we admit the exact nature of our wrongs. It is not necessary to discuss how the wrongs came about or how changes will be made. You are not seeking counsel or advice.

- As the listener, be patient and accepting. You are God's spokesperson and are communicating God's unconditional acceptance.

- As the listener you are there to help the communicator express thoughts clearly. Ask questions when necessary so the information can be clearly understood by both of you.

- When Step Five is completed, both parties can share their feelings about the experience. It is now possible to extend to each other the love God extends to us through Christ Jesus.

- Observe confidentiality. What you have shared is personal. Nothing defeats honesty and damages relationships faster than a betrayed confidence.

The following information is helpful when completing your Fifth Step with God:

- Step Five is for your own benefit—God already knows you. You are beginning a process of living a life of humility, honesty and courage. The result is freedom, happiness and serenity.

- Start with prayer; e.g., "Lord, I understand that you already know me completely. I am now ready to openly and humbly reveal myself to you—my hurtful behaviors, self-centeredness and traits. I am grateful to you for the gifts and abilities that have brought me to this point in my life. Take away my fear of being known and rejected. I place myself and my life in your care and keeping."

- Speak out loud, sincerely and honestly sharing your understanding of the insights you gained from your Fourth Step inventory. Be aware that emotions may surface as part of the powerful cleansing experience taking place.

- The objective is balance. Remember that each of your character traits has a strength and a weakness. Begin with resentments and fears. Then proceed to those traits you have included in your Fourth Step Inventory.

The following information is helpful when completing your Fifth Step with yourself:

- Writing your Fourth Step inventory began the process of developing your self-awareness, the first step toward what will become genuine self-love. Solitary self-appraisal is the beginning of your confession, but it is insufficient in itself. The Fifth Step is where you turn that knowledge into enhanced self-acceptance.

- Sit in a chair with your imaginary double seated across from you in an empty chair. Or sit in front of a mirror that allows you to see yourself as you speak.

- Speak out loud. Allow yourself time to hear what you are saying, and to note any deeper understanding that occurs.

- Acknowledge your courage for proceeding to this point. This and every part of this process releases excess emotional baggage that you have carried around because of low self-worth.

The following information is helpful when completing your Fifth Step with another person:

- Simply stated, it takes considerable humility to bare ourselves to another person. We are about to reveal our self-defeating, damaging and harmful character traits, we will also disclose our positive and contributing traits. We must do this to remove the stage-character masks we present to the world. It is a bold step toward eliminating our need for pretense and hiding.

- Review the guidelines for choosing your Fifth Step listener when selecting a person to assist you in completing your Fifth Step. Begin your sharing with the **Resentment** and **Fear Exercises** in your workbook and then proceed by disclosing the character traits you wrote about.

You may never see that person again, which is okay. It is your decision to continue the relationship in whatever direction you choose, from casual friendship to deeper spiritual companionship.

After completing your Fifth Step, take time for prayer and meditation to reflect on what you have done. Thank God for the tool you have been given to improve your relationship with Him. Spend time rereading the first five Steps and note anything you have omitted. Acknowledge that you are laying a new foundation for your life. The cornerstone is your relationship with God and your commitment to honesty and humility.

Congratulate yourself for having the courage to risk self-disclosure, and thank God for the peace of mind you have achieved.

Notes: _____

_____

_____

_____

_____

_____

_____

_____

_____

_____

_____

_____

_____

_____

_____

_____

_____

_____

_____

_____

_____

_____

_____

_____

_____

_____

_____

_____

_____

_____

_____

_____

_____

STEP SIX

*Were entirely ready to have God remove all
these defects of character.*

Humble yourselves before the
Lord, and he will lift you up.
(James 4:10)

Having completed Steps One through Five, some of us may believe that we can stop here. The truth is, that much more work lies ahead, and the best results are yet to come. In Steps One and Two, we recognized our powerlessness and came to believe in a Power greater than ourselves. In Step Three, we turned our wills and our lives over to God's care. Steps Four and Five created an atmosphere for developing self-awareness and humility by admitting our wrongs to God, to ourselves, and to another person. This foundation for recovery that we have built may create the illusion that everything is okay and that the remaining Steps may be marginally relevant. If we believe this, we will surely undermine our spiritual growth, as many of us have.

Actually, Steps One through Five helped us to steer in the right direction as we built our foundation for ultimate surrender. Approaching Step Six, we are confronted with the need to change our attitudes and lifestyles. Here, we prepare to make these changes and totally alter the course of our lives.

The changes that are about to take place in our lives will result from a cooperative effort— God provides the direction while we provide the desire and action. All we need is the willingness to let God lead our journey. He never forces Himself on us. We must invite Him into our lives, content in knowing that He will never leave or forsake us.

We are not expected to remove our character defects alone; we are expected only to let go and let God. Step Six is not an action step that we actually take. It is a state of being that enables us to release our faults to God. As our willingness to surrender increases, we will reach the point where we are ready to let God take over and remove our defects as He sees fit. We do this by working the Program, one day at a time, whether or not we can see that we are making any progress.

We must remind ourselves that the character traits we want to eliminate are often deeply ingrained patterns of behavior, developed through many years of struggling to survive. They will not vanish overnight. We must be patient while God is shaping us into new people. Through this willingness to let God be in control, we learn to trust Him more completely.

Step Six is similar to Step Two. Both Steps deal with our willingness to allow God to work through us to change our lives. In Step Two, we are seeking our restoration to sanity by coming to believe in a Power greater than ourselves. In Step Six, we are seeking total readiness to let God remove our defects of character. Both Steps acknowledge the existence of problems and require that we seek God's help in being freed from them. The fact that we "came to believe" will strengthen our capacity to be "entirely ready."

Personal Reflection

To be successful with Step Six, we must sincerely desire to change our disabling behaviors. Our past has been dominated by our self-will, through which we sought to control our environment. We victimized ourselves by our self-will, rarely calling on God for help. By recognizing our life condition and being honestly determined to eliminate our behavior flaws, we see that self-will has never been enough to help us. We must be ready to accept help and relinquish our self-destructive natures.

- Explain your commitment to changing your behavior. What are you willing to do to change? _____

_____

_____

_____

1 PETER 1:13-14
> *Therefore, prepare your minds for action; be self-controlled; set your hope fully on the grace to be given you when Jesus Christ is revealed.*

- What do you feel when you think of surrendering to Christ and trusting that He will remove your defects? _____

_____

_____

_____

◆ ◆ ◆

At this point in our Program, we see that change is necessary to live life to the fullest. Recognizing the need for change and being willing to change are two different matters. The space between recognition and willingness to change can be filled with fear. As we move toward willingness, we must let go of our fears and remain secure in the knowledge that with God's guidance everything will be restored to us. When we are "entirely ready," we begin to see the possibilities available to us once we change our behavior. The excitement of this revelation will help us do whatever may be necessary to achieve the results we want. From now on, there will be no turning back.

- What is your interpretation of "there will be no turning back?" _____

_____

_____

_____

PSALM 37:4-5
> *Delight yourself in the LORD and he will give you the desires of your heart. Commit your way to the LORD; trust in him and he will do this:*

● Cite examples that indicate you are committing your way to the care and guidance of the Lord. _____

_____

_____

_____

PHILIPPIANS 3:12-14

Not that I have already obtained all this, or have already been made perfect, but I press on to take hold of that for which Christ Jesus took hold of me. Brothers, I do not consider myself yet to have taken hold of it. But one thing I do: Forgetting what is behind and straining toward what is ahead, I press on toward the goal to win the prize for which God has called me heavenward in Christ Jesus.

● In which areas do you have to work the hardest to give up your defects? _____

_____

_____

_____

◆ ◆ ◆

In preparing to have our character defects removed, we will see that they are familiar tools to us, and losing them threatens our capacity to control ourselves and others. We can trust that God won't remove anything we need. This creates in us a beginning sense of comfort. The smallest beginning is acceptable to God. Scripture tells us that if we have "faith as small as a mustard seed" nothing is impossible for us (Matthew 17:30). When we have planted our seed of willingness, we need to look for and protect the tiny sprouts of positive results. We do not want the weeds of self-will to overrun our new garden. These seedlings of "willingness" respond quickly to our nurturing.

● What anxieties do you feel when considering having your character defects removed? __

_____

_____

_____

● Identify any character defects you are not entirely ready to have removed. Explain why you are attached to them. _____

_____

_____

_____

ROMANS 12:2

Do not conform any longer to the pattern of this world, but be transformed by the renewing of your mind. Then you will be able to test and approve what God's will is—his good, pleasing and perfect will.

● In what ways are you testing and approving what God's will is doing in your life? _____

_____

_____

_____

◆ ◆ ◆

Our ability to talk to God is an important part of Step Six. We need to communicate with God in a way that shows our humility and invites His intervention. When we say, "Dear God, I want to be more patient," we are making a demand and telling God what we want. When we say "Dear God, I am impatient," we present the truth about ourselves. This allows God to manifest our behavior change based on our admission of error. When we pray in this manner, we exhibit humility, relinquish our pride and ask God to act on our behalf.

- List examples of your prayers that show you are making demands on God, rather than asking for His will to be done in your life. _____

_____

_____

_____

JAMES 4:10

Humble yourselves before the Lord, and he will lift you up.

- Why is it necessary to learn humility before God can remove your defects of character?

_____

_____

_____

JAMES 1:5-6

If any of you lacks wisdom, he should ask God, who gives generously to all without finding fault, and it will be given to him. But when he asks, he must believe and not doubt, because he who doubts is like a wave of the sea, blown and tossed by the wind.

- List any doubts you have that are interfering with your readiness to have God remove your shortcomings. _____

_____

_____

_____

◆ ◆ ◆

This Step requires that we look at those defects of character we will ask to have removed. We may be unwilling to give up some of them. They may seem useful to us, so we respond, "I cannot give up...yet." We have a potential problem if we say "I will never be any different, and will never give up..." These attitudes shut our mind to God's saving grace and can precipitate our destruction. If we respond this way to any behavior, we need to renew our trust in God and recommit ourselves to doing His will.

- How will your trust in God help you give up your destructive behavior? _____

_____

_____

_____

● What do you fear will happen when your defects are removed? _____

_____

_____

_____

2 THESSALONIANS 3:3
But the Lord is faithful, and he will strengthen and protect you from the evil one.

● How is the Lord strengthening and protecting you now? _____

_____

_____

_____

◆ ◆ ◆

As we follow the principles of the Program in our daily lives, we gradually and unconsciously prepare to have our shortcomings removed. Sometimes, we are even unaware of our readiness to have our defects removed. At first, we realize that we are behaving differently—that we have changed. Sometimes, others note the changes before we become aware of them ourselves. Approval-seekers begin to function more independently; control addicts become more easygoing and more relaxed; caretakers become more sensitive to their own needs. People who diligently work the Program as an integral part of their lives become calmer, more serene, and genuinely happy.

● What behavioral changes have you made that indicate your thought patterns are chang-

ing? _____

_____

_____

_____

ROMANS 6:11-12
In the same way, count yourselves dead to sin but alive to God in Christ Jesus. Therefore do not let sin reign in your mortal body so that you obey its evil desires.

● Which character defects have caused the most pain and need to be removed first? _____

_____

_____

_____

◆ ◆ ◆

A radiant, confident person lives in each of us, hidden under a cloud of confusion and uncertainty, distracted by ineffective behavior. If someone asked us if we wanted to be freed from our character defects, we could give only one answer—we are entirely ready to have God remove them.

- What does being "entirely ready" mean to you? _____

_____

_____

_____

PSALM 119:10-12

I seek you with all my heart; do not let me stray from your commands. I have hidden your word in my heart that I might not sin against you. Praise be to you, O LORD; teach me your decrees.

- How will seeking God's will with all your heart make it easier for you to be entirely ready

  to have your character defects removed? _____

_____

_____

_____

1 JOHN 5:14-15

This is the assurance we have in approaching God: that is if we ask anything according to his will, he hears us. And if we know that he hears us—whatever we ask—we know that we have what we asked of him.

- Describe your level of assurance that God will remove your defects of character. _____

_____

_____

_____

◆ ◆ ◆

READINESS EXERCISE

The following exercise is intended to help you prepare to let go of the character defects you discovered when working Step Four. When necessary, refer to your Fourth Step written inventory.

Pride: Inordinate conceit; disdainful behavior or treatment of others.

- List examples that indicate you are willing to let go of your constant need to impress others. _____

_____

_____

_____

- What difficulty are you having in letting go of your preoccupation with self? _____

_____

_____

_____

Greed: Selfishness; excessive acquisitiveness; never having enough of anything.

- What do you fear you will lose by letting go of your intense desire for material things?

_____

_____

_____

- What will you gain by giving up your selfish tendencies? _____

_____

_____

_____

Lust: Lechery; an intense indulgence in inappropriate sexual activity.

- What inappropriate sexual behavior will you be giving up? _____

_____

_____

_____

- How will removing your lustful tendencies change your current social behavior? _____

_____

_____

_____

Dishonesty: Deceit: disposition to defraud to deceive; justifying behaviors by explaining ourselves dishonestly.

- What anxieties do you feel when you realize the need to tell the truth? _____

  _____

  _____

  _____

- How will honesty improve the quality of your life? _____

  _____

  _____

  _____

Gluttony: Covetousness; one given habitually to greedy or voracious acquisition of possessions; excessive eating or drinking.

- In the process of changing your habits of over-indulgence, what benefits do you hope to receive? _____

  _____

  _____

  _____

- What are you ready to give up? _____

  _____

  _____

  _____

Envy: Jealousy; painful or resentful longing for an advantage or benefit enjoyed by another, joined with a desire to possess the same perceived benefit.

- In what ways are you ready to lessen your desires for status and material wealth? _____

  _____

  _____

  _____

- What do you believe your life will be like when you no longer experience jealousy? _____

  _____

  _____

  _____

Laziness: Disinclined to activity or exertion; not energetic or vigorous; distinct avoidance of responsibility.

- List examples that indicate you are willing to heighten your productivity. _____

  _____

  _____

  _____

- What steps have you taken to eliminate your habit of procrastination? _____

  _____

  _____

  _____

Notes: _____

_____

_____

_____

_____

_____

_____

_____

_____

_____

_____

_____

_____

_____

_____

_____

_____

_____

_____

_____

_____

_____

_____

_____

_____

_____

_____

_____

_____

_____

_____

_____

_____

_____

_____

_____

STEP SEVEN

Humbly asked Him to remove our shortcomings.

*If we confess our sins, he is faithful and just and will forgive
us our sins and purify us from all unrighteousness.*

(1 John 1:9)

Humility is a recurring theme in the Twelve Step Program and the central idea of Step Seven. By practicing humility we receive the strength necessary to work the Program and achieve satisfactory results. We recognize now, more than ever before, that a major portion of our lives has been devoted to fulfilling our self-centered desires. We must set aside these prideful, selfish behavior patterns, come to terms with our inadequacies and realize that humility alone will free our spirit. Step Seven requires surrendering our will to God so that we may receive the serenity necessary to achieve the happiness we seek.

We are growing in wisdom and understanding, not only as a result of our seeking it, but also from the insight we have gained by examining the pain of our past struggles. We gain greater courage by hearing how others have coped with their life challenges. As we work through the Steps, we begin to recognize the value of acknowledging the truth of our past. Although the pain of this reality may seem to be unbearable, the insights we achieve are the only means to our release.

Step Six prepared us to let go of our old defective behavior patterns and develop the powerful new ones that God intends for us to use. Asking God to remove our defects is a true measure of our willingness to surrender control. For those of us who have spent our lives thinking we were self-sufficient, it can be an extremely difficult task, but not an impossible one. If we are sincerely ready to abandon these deceptions, we can then ask God to be instrumental in letting go of our past and in the creation of our new life.

Step Seven is the first and most important part of the cleansing process and prepares us for the next stage of our journey. During the first six Steps, we became aware of our desperate situation, looked at our lives honestly, disclosed previously hidden aspects of ourselves and became ready to change our attitudes and behaviors. Step Seven presents us with the opportunity to turn to God and ask for removal of those parts of our character that cause us pain.

Prior to beginning this Program, we avoided ever looking at ourselves honestly and admitting the extent of our disabling behavior. Meditating on Christ's presence in our lives will focus our attention on living life according to His example and free us from this disabling burden of ''self.'' Our partnership with Christ will increase our concern for the whole human family and put our obsession with ''self'' into its proper perspective. We will finally recognize the person we have been, understand who we are now and look forward with joy to the persons we are becoming.

Preparing to have our defects removed requires our willingness to work with God to revise and redirect our attention and activity. Our progress will be halted if we continue our destructive behavior patterns. We must be ever-vigilant and alert to the possible return of "old behaviors" and work diligently toward eliminating them from our frame of reference. It is wise to be gentle with ourselves and remember that it took us a lifetime to develop these habits. It is not realistic to expect them to disappear overnight.

When looking to God to remove our shortcomings, we must realize that God gives grace through other people as well as directly to us through prayer and meditation. God often uses outside forces to correct our defects. Ministers, teachers, medical doctors and therapists can all be instruments of God's grace. Our willingness to seek outside help can be a clear indication of our readiness to change. Compulsive worriers can pray to God to release their worries and, at the same time, seek help from a counselor to relieve their anxiety. Persons who over-indulge in food or drugs can seek professional help to gain control over their obsessive habits. We need to pray for God's help in removing our shortcomings, and have the courage to seek appropriate professional help when we know we need it.

Personal Reflection

Through working the Steps, we are progressing toward a happier and healthier life. We see how the opportunities and blessings that God brings into our lives surpass anything we could ever have created on our own. Having completed the first six Steps, we are becoming aware of the multitude of benefits available to us. Through this awareness, we become grateful for God's presence and secure in the knowledge that our lives are improving.

- What benefits are you receiving from God's presence in your life? _____
  _____
  _____
  _____

- What special blessings has God sent to you since you began your Twelve Step Program of recovery? _____
  _____
  _____
  _____

PSALM 25:8-11

> Good and upright is the LORD; therefore he instructs sinners in his ways. He guides the humble in what is right and teaches them his way. All the ways of the LORD are loving and faithful for those who keep the demands of his covenant. For the sake of your name, O LORD, forgive my iniquity, though it is great.

- How is God guiding you and teaching you what is right? _____
  _____
  _____
  _____

♦ ♦ ♦

Step Seven implies that we ask for removal of all our shortcomings. However, the process will be more manageable if we deal with them individually, working on the easiest ones first to build up our confidence and strength. If we are patient, God will see that we achieve our goal at a pace that is comfortable for us. Our willingness to accept God's help builds our trust and encourages the growth of confidence in ourselves and in God. If we ask God to relieve us of a burdensome behavior pattern and it doesn't seem to go away, we need to work harder on our willingness to release it. Becoming angry or discouraged is self-defeating. When things do not seem to be going according to our timetable, reciting the Serenity Prayer can work to our advantage.

- List areas in which you are discouraged about your level of progress in having your defects removed. _____

_____

_____

_____

PHILIPPIANS 4:6

Do not be anxious about anything, but in everything, by prayer and petition, with thanksgiving, present your requests to God.

- In what way does prayer relieve your feelings of anxiety? _____

_____

_____

_____

1 JOHN 1:9

If we confess our sins, he is faithful and just and will forgive us our sins and purify us from all unrighteousness.

- How will confessing our sins purify us from all unrighteousness? _____

_____

_____

_____

♦ ♦ ♦

Letting go of negative behavior patterns, however destructive they are, may create a sense of loss and require that we allow ourselves time to grieve. It is normal to grieve for the loss of something we no longer have. If, however, in our childhood we experienced "things" being taken from us abruptly or before we were ready to release them, we may now be overly sensitive and may cling to "things" to avoid the pain of loss. Rather than using our own ineffective strategies to avoid or deny the existence of our fear of giving up, we can turn to our Lord for courage and trust the outcome. Even though our childhood learning did not adequately prepare us for grieving the adult losses we must handle, our love and trust in God can heal our memories, repair the damage and restore us to wholeness.

- What "things" were taken away from you as a child before you were ready to give them up? _____

_____

_____

_____

MATTHEW 23:12
For whoever exalts himself will be humbled, and whoever humbles himself will be exalted.

● List examples that indicate you are practicing humility. _____

_____

_____

_____

◆ ◆ ◆

Changing our behavior can be temporarily alarming to our sense of self. Our fear of not knowing what is ahead may cause us to repeat past destructive actions. We may retreat into feeling isolated and lose our sense of belonging. Having faith and trusting in our relationship with God is an indication of our willingness to release the fear of being lost, frightened, or abandoned.

● What do you fear by not knowing what lies ahead? _____

_____

_____

_____

JAMES 4:6-8
But he gives us more grace. That is why Scripture says: "God opposes the proud but gives grace to the humble." Submit yourselves, then, to God. Resist the devil, and he will flee from you. Come near to God and he will come near to you. Wash your hands, you sinners, and purify your hearts, you double-minded.

● Describe your present relationship with God. _____

_____

_____

_____

◆ ◆ ◆

As we begin to see our defects being removed and our lives becoming less complicated, we must proceed with caution and guard against the temptation to be prideful. Sudden changes in our behavior can and do happen, but we cannot anticipate them or direct them. God initiates change when we are ready, and we cannot claim that we alone removed our character defects. When we learn to ask humbly for God's help in our lives, change becomes God's responsibility, and we cannot accept the credit.

● Cite examples that indicate you are focusing more on God and less on yourself? _____

_____

_____

_____

PSALM 51:10-12
Create in me a pure heart, O God, and renew a steadfast spirit within me. Do not cast me from your presence or take your Holy Spirit from me. Restore to me the joy of your salvation and grant me a willing spirit, to sustain me.

● How do you feel cast away from God's presence? How will turning to God help correct this? _____

_____

_____

_____

◆ ◆ ◆

Destructive behavior patterns that remain with us after we complete Step Seven may never be eliminated, but may have to be transformed. We have an opportunity to transform these aspects of our character into positive traits and learn to use them in a healthy way. Leaders may be left with a quest for power but with no desire to misuse it. Lovers will be left with exquisite sensuality, but with enough sensitivity to refrain from causing pain to the person they love. Those who are materially wealthy may continue to be, but will set aside their greed and possessiveness. With the help of Our Lord, all aspects of our personal life can be rewarding. By continuing to practice humility and accept the tools God is giving us, we will eventually begin to aspire to a more Christ-like life, sharing with others the love we have received.

● Which of your negative character traits are becoming positive? Explain how this change is making an impact on your life. _____

_____

_____

_____

◆ ◆ ◆

1 PETER 5:6-7
Humble yourselves, therefore, under God's mighty hand, that he may lift you up in due time. Cast all your anxiety on him because he cares for you.

● How has humbling yourself before the Lord helped you to acknowledge that He can remove your shortcomings? _____

_____

_____

_____

◆ ◆ ◆

In order for the Program to be successful, we must practice the Steps on a daily basis. When we have moments of inner struggle, we can simply say "This too will pass"; "I let go and let God"; "I fear no evil"; "I choose to see the good in this experience." Whatever affirmation we use, its power keeps us from reverting to our obsessive/compulsive behavior. Depression, guilt and anger can be acknowledged and understood to be temporary.

● What affirmations do you use as a part of your ongoing commitment to recovery? _____

_____

_____

_____

PSALM 51:1-2

Have mercy on me, O God, according to your unfailing love; according to your great compassion blot out my transgressions. Wash away all my iniquity and cleanse me from my sin.

- How is God being merciful to you? _____
  _____
  _____
  _____

◆ ◆ ◆

We need to stop for a moment and acknowledge ourselves for our commitment to recovery. Note how our determination enables us to break the bonds of our unhealthy habits and behaviors. Accept the positive, spontaneous thoughts and feelings that occur and see that this results from our personal relationship with God. We learn that the guidance we receive from our Lord is always available; all we need to do is listen, receive and act without fear.

- List examples of your behavior that indicate you have the courage to change the things
  you can. _____
  _____
  _____
  _____

ACTS 3:19

Repent, then, and turn to God, so that your sins may be wiped out, that times of refreshing may come from the Lord.

- What changes in behavior have occurred as a result of working Step Seven? _____
  _____
  _____
  _____

PRAYER FOR SERENITY

God, grant me the serenity
to accept the things I cannot change,
the courage to change the things I can,
and the wisdom to know the difference.
Living one day at a time,
enjoying one moment at a time;
accepting hardship as a pathway to peace;
taking, as Jesus did,
this sinful world as it is,
not as I would have it;
trusting that You will make all things right
if I surrender to your will;
so that I may be reasonably happy in this life
and supremely happy with You forever in the next.
AMEN
Reinhold Niebuhr

TRAIT REMOVAL EXERCISE

The following exercise is intended to help you review your success in letting go of your character defects.

Humility: Being aware of one's shortcomings; not proud; not aggressive; modest.

- List ways in which you are practicing humility. _____
_____
_____
_____

- How has humility helped your willingness to have God remove your shortcomings? _____
_____
_____
_____

Generosity: Willingness to give or share; being unselfish.

- Cite examples of your willingness to share with others. _____
_____
_____
_____

- How does your new behavior help you to care about the happiness and welfare of others?
_____
_____
_____

Acceptance of Sexual Self: Feeling comfortable with your sexual nature, without needing to have it lead to sexual intercourse. Clearly expressing preferences for sexual activity with partner.

- How has your sexual behavior improved as a result of letting go of your inappropriate sexual relating? _____
_____
_____
_____

- How has your self-esteem been enhanced because of your improved sexuality? _____
_____
_____
_____

Honesty: Telling the truth; being trustworthy.

- What feelings surface when you risk being honest in your communication with other people? _____

_____

_____

_____

- How has being trustworthy improved your relationship with others? _____

_____

_____

_____

Temperance: Moderation in eating and drinking; control of self-indulgence in all things.

- Cite examples which indicate moderation in your use of food and drink. _____

_____

_____

_____

- How do you control self-indulgence in other areas? _____

_____

_____

_____

Amicable: Friendly; harmonious; enthusiastic and helpful toward others.

- How has being friendly helped you to feel more comfortable with yourself and others?

_____

_____

_____

- List ways in which your enthusiasm toward others is improving your self-confidence. ___

_____

_____

_____

Energetic: Active interest in ideas and activities; attention to needs at work and play.

● In what areas of your life has increased energy been most rewarding? _____

_____

_____

_____

● Cite examples of your work habits that indicate you are being more productive. _____

_____

_____

_____

SEVENTH STEP PRAYER

My Creator, I am now willing
that you should have all of me,
good and bad.
I pray that you now remove from me
every single defect of character
which stands in the way of
my usefulness to you and my fellows.
Grant me the strength,
as I go out from here,
to do your bidding.
AMEN[1]

Big Book (A.A.)

[1]Alcoholics Anonymous, Alcoholics Anonymous World Services, Inc. (New York), p. 76.

SERENITY PRAYER EXERCISE

The following examples are intended to help you in using the Serenity Prayer as part of your ongoing recovery process. It is a tool that can be used daily when seeking God's help. The exercise gives you an opportunity to take a situation through the Serenity Prayer.

God, grant me the serenity to accept the things I cannot change . . . . like the way_____ignores me, especially when I want praise

the courage to change the things I can . . especially my own character defects and feelings toward myself for never having enough approval from people I admire

and the wisdom to know the difference . . between the lasting satisfaction of reparenting myself with approval and the temporary satisfaction of depending on _____ for it.

God, grant me the serenity to accept the things I cannot change . . . . like the way my childhood was

the courage to change the things I can . . especially my own victimized feelings about my childhood

and the wisdom to know the difference . . between staying in a victim role and continually turning those years over to God.

God, grant me the serenity to accept the things I cannot change . . . . like my parents' incompatability with each other

the courage to change the things I can . . especially my feelings of abandonment, anger, isolation

and the wisdom to know the difference . . between my parents' love being unavailable to me and God's love which is always with me.

Select a specific situation or condition in your life that is currently a source of resentment, fear, sadness or anger. It may involve relationships (family, work or sexual), work environment, health or self-esteem.

God, grant me the serenity to accept the things I cannot change

- State the condition or experience you are aware of that you cannot change (e.g., childhood, partner's behavior, employment conditions, parents' behavior). _____
_____
_____
_____

The courage to change the things I can

- Indicate the specific condition or situation that you believe can be changed. _____
_____
_____
_____

And the wisdom to know the difference

- Identify your understanding and acceptance of what you can and cannot change (e.g., frozen feelings vs. flowing feelings; anger vs. peace). _____
_____
_____
_____

- List any insights gained from this exercise. _____
_____
_____
_____

Notes: _____

_____

_____

_____

_____

_____

_____

_____

_____

_____

_____

_____

_____

_____

_____

_____

_____

_____

_____

_____

_____

_____

_____

_____

_____

_____

_____

_____

_____

STEP EIGHT

*Made a list of all persons we had harmed, and
became willing to make amends to them all.*

Do to others as you would have them do to you.
(Luke 6:31)

Prior to entering the Twelve Step Program, many of us blamed our parents, relatives and friends for the turmoil in our lives. We even held God responsible. In Step Eight, we begin the process of releasing the need to blame others for our misfortune and accepting full responsibility for our own lives. Our Fourth Step inventory revealed that our inappropriate behavior caused injury not only to us, but also to the significant others in our lives. Now we must prepare to accept full responsibility and make amends.

Steps One through Seven helped us to center ourselves in the healing power of Jesus Christ, and started the process of getting our lives in order. We were given the tools to examine our personal experiences and to see the importance of letting go of the past; thus becoming free to continue our personal growth. We must not be deterred by the pain of our past mistakes. Our personal progress is directly related to our success in facing our history and putting it behind us. Like barnacles on a ship's hull, our past wrongdoings prevent us from sailing smoothly to a life filled with peace.

Working Steps Eight and Nine will improve our relationships, both with ourselves and others, and lead us out of isolation and loneliness. The key factor here is our willingness to make amends to those whom we have harmed. As we continue to welcome Christ's presence into our hearts, we will develop a new openness with others that prepares us for the face-to-face admission of our past misconduct. In Step Eight, we examine each past misdeed and identify the persons involved. Our intention is to make amends in order to heal our past so that God can transform the present.

Reviewing our Fourth Step inventory will help us determine who belongs on our list. Preparing to make amends is a difficult task—one that we will execute with increasing skill, yet never really finish. Again, uncomfortable feelings may surface as we come to grips with our past behaviors. As we recognize the damage caused by our actions, we will glimpse the great relief that we will feel when we no longer cause injury to ourselves and others.

For many of us, admitting our misdeeds will be difficult. The pattern of our lives has been to blame others and to seek retribution for the wrongs done to us, rather than to admit we have initiated harm. As we become willing to look at ourselves, we see that, in many cases, the retribution we vainly sought just created more havoc. By insisting on our own measure of justice, we lost the ability to set and achieve positive goals. Cycles of hatred and hard feelings were created, and we kept our attention focused away from ourselves.

Forgiving ourselves and others helps us overcome our resentments. God has already forgiven us for the harmful actions that separated us from Him. Developing the ability to forgive ourselves is an important element in our ongoing recovery. To do so, we first must accept responsibility for the harm done and make amends with dignity and self-respect. Making amends without personally extending our forgiveness leads to dishonesty and further complicates our lives.

To repair our past wrongdoings, we must be willing to face them by recording the harm we think we have caused. When preparing the list of people whom we have harmed, we must sustain thoughts that enable us to initiate reconciliation, even though our intentions may be rebuffed. In some cases, people on our list feel bitter toward us and may resist our attempts at restitution. They may hold deep grudges and be unwilling to reconcile with us. Regardless of how we are received, we must be willing to forgive. We must remember that the list we make is principally for our own benefit, not the benefit of those whom we have harmed.

Personal Reflection

Step Eight begins the process of healing damaged relationships through our willingness to make amends for past misdeeds. We can let go of our resentments and start to overcome the guilt, shame and low self-esteem we have acquired through our harmful actions. We can leave the gray, angry world of loneliness behind and move toward a bright future by exercising our newly developed relating skills. Through the gift of the Steps, we have the necessary tools to overcome these damaging conditions and mend our broken friendships.

- List the relationships most severely damaged by your past misdeeds. _____

_____

_____

_____

- How will making amends help free you from resentment, guilt and shame? _____

_____

_____

_____

LUKE 19:8

> But Zacchaeus stood up and said to the Lord, "Look, Lord! Here and now I give half of my possessions to the poor, and if I have cheated anybody out of anything, I will pay back four times the amount."

- List situations in which you have cheated others. How will you make restitution? _____

_____

_____

_____

◆ ◆ ◆

As Christians, we are taught the importance of having and maintaining deep, loving relationships. Through Christ's example, we see how He devoted His ministry to loving people and encouraging them to love one another. Jesus taught that being reconciled to God requires reconciliation with other human beings. In Step Eight, we prepare ourselves to carry out God's master plan for our lives by becoming willing to make amends. Once we have prepared our list of those whom we have harmed, we will be able to extend our love and acceptance not only to the injured persons, but also to all other members of God's family.

- Why does reconciliation with God require reconciliation with others? _____

_____

_____

_____

1 JOHN 4:11-12

Dear friends, since God so loved us, we also ought to love one another. No one has ever seen God; but if we love one another, God lives in us and his love is made complete in us.

- How does God's love for you enable you to love others? _____

_____

_____

_____

MATTHEW 6:14-15

For if you forgive men when they sin against you, your heavenly Father will also forgive you. But if you do not forgive men their sins, your Father will not forgive your sins.

- How does your unwillingness to forgive others block your progress and hurt your re-

lationship with God? _____

_____

_____

_____

ROMANS 2:1

You, therefore, have no excuse, you who pass judgment on someone else, for at whatever point you judge the other, you are condemning yourself, because you who pass judgment do the same things.

_____

- Cite an example of your passing judgment on others and harming them and yourself.

_____

_____

_____

◆ ◆ ◆

Forgiveness is a two-way street. As Christ declared in the Lord's Prayer: "Forgive us our trespasses, as we forgive those who trespass against us..."; we need to ask forgiveness of those whom we have harmed, as we forgive those who have harmed us. As we reflect on our Lord, we see how He encourages us to "turn the other cheek," to love our enemies and pray for our persecutors. Only in this manner can we break the cycle of hatred and violence.

- How will making amends help you to forgive others and free you from your past? _____

_____

_____

_____

LUKE 6: 27-31

> *"But I tell you who hear me: Love your enemies, do good to those who hate you, bless those who curse you, pray for those who mistreat you. If someone strikes you on one cheek, turn to him the other also. If someone takes your cloak, do not stop him from taking your tunic. Give to everyone who asks you, and if anyone takes what belongs to you, do not demand it back. Do to others as you would have them do to you."*

- Cite examples of your behavior that indicate you are willing to love your enemies. _____

_____

_____

_____

◆ ◆ ◆

When making our list, we need to examine our relationships with people at home, in our community and in the world at large. We must learn to forgive, and to accept the grace that comes as a part of such forgiveness. If we ask God to help us, our task will be much easier. We can ask Him for guidance in determining the names of the persons with whom we need to communicate. Setting aside our pride will help us see that all thoughts and feelings have worth and value. We do not have to agree with everyone, nor must they agree with us, but we can stop hating people for what they think and do—resenting them because their views are different from ours.

- How will Step Eight improve your relationships with others? _____

_____

_____

_____

- List three personal experiences that require making amends. _____

_____

_____

_____

LUKE 6:37-38

> *"Do not judge, and you will not be judged. Do not condemn, and you will not be condemned. Forgive, and you will be forgiven. Give, and it will be given to you. A good measure, pressed down, shaken together and running over, will be poured into your lap. For with the measure you use, it will be measured to you.*

- What do you expect to gain by giving to others? _____

_____

_____

_____

◆ ◆ ◆

In some cases, we will be prevented from facing the people on our list directly. They may be deceased, separated from us or unwilling to meet with us. Whatever the situation, we still need to put them on our list. When we actually make the amends in Step Nine, we will see why amends are necessary, even if they cannot be face-to-face. Being willing to make the amend will release us from hard feelings and enable us to experience serenity and peace of mind.

- What do you hope to accomplish by making amends? _____

_____

_____

_____

EPHESIANS 4:32
Be kind and compassionate to one another, forgiving each other, just as in Christ God forgave you.

- In what ways are you compassionate toward those who have caused you harm? _____

_____

_____

_____

◆ ◆ ◆

When looking at those persons whom we have harmed, we see how our character defects have played a major part in sabotaging our lives and our relationships. Examples of this behavior are:

- When we became angry, we often harmed ourselves more than others. This may have resulted in feelings of depression or self-pity.

- Persistent financial problems resulting from our irresponsible actions caused difficulty with our family and creditors.

- When confronted with an issue about which we felt guilty, we lashed out at others rather than looking honestly at ourselves.

- Frustrated by our lack of control, we behaved aggressively and intimidated those around us.

- Because of our indiscriminate sexual behavior, true intimacy was impossible to achieve or maintain.

- Our fear of abandonment sometimes destroyed our relationships, because we did not allow others to be themselves. We created dependency and tried to control their behavior in an effort to maintain the relationship we wanted it to be.

- What major character defects caused injury to yourself or others? _____

_____

_____

_____

- What consequences do you fear in making your amends? _____

_____

_____

_____

ROMANS 15:1-3
We who are strong ought to bear with the failings of the weak and not to please ourselves. Each of us should please his neighbor for his good, to build him up. For even Christ did not please himself, but, as it is written: "The insults of those who insult you have fallen on me."

- How will loving your neighbors build them up and be a means of making restitution? __

  _____

  _____

  _____

♦ ♦ ♦

When making a list of people to whom making an amend is necessary, we need to remember to focus on ourselves. As adult children, many of us have been victims of self-inflicted pain because we did not have the skills to take care of ourselves appropriately. We spent time and energy trying to be available for everybody and sacrificed ourselves in the process. We may have become our own worst enemy and experienced excessive self-blame, guilt and shame. Taking time to look at the harm we have inflicted upon ourselves and being willing to forgive ourselves is essential to our continued growth.

- Why is forgiving yourself an important factor in the amends making process? _____

  _____

  _____

  _____

- List the major ways in which you have harmed yourself. _____

  _____

  _____

  _____

MATTHEW 7:3-4

"Why do you look at the speck of sawdust in your brother's eye and pay no attention to the plank in your own eye? How can you say to your brother, 'Let me take the speck out of your eye,' when all the time there is a plank in your own eye?"

- List situations in which you worried about others, when it would have been healthier to focus on what was happening to you. _____

  _____

  _____

  _____

♦ ♦ ♦

In Step Nine, we will seek out the people whom we have harmed, and make amends wherever necessary. For now, all we need to do is list them and describe the harmful behavior. The consequences of our actions may have produced emotional, financial or physical pain to others. We need to take as much time as necessary to reflect on our list and be as thorough as possible. Being totally honest with ourselves is a major factor in our ability to make restitution for our past destructive actions.

● Examine your list and identify your behavior that produced emotional, financial or physical pain. _____

_____

_____

_____

MARK 11:25

"And when you stand praying, if you hold anything against anyone, forgive him, so that your Father in heaven may forgive you your sins."

● How will your recovery be hindered if you are unwilling to forgive others? _____

_____

_____

_____

◆ ◆ ◆

AMENDS LIST GUIDELINES

The following are three main categories in which we may have caused harm and for which we must be willing to make amends.

Material Wrongs: Actions which affected an individual in a tangible way, such as:

- Borrowing or spending extravagance; stinginess; spending in an attempt to buy friendship or love; withholding money in order to gratify yourself.

- Entering into agreements that are legally enforceable, then refusing to abide by the terms or simply cheating.

- Injuring or damaging persons or property as a result of our actions.

Moral Wrongs: Inappropriate behavior in moral or ethical actions and conduct, including questions of rightness, fairness or equity. The principal issue is involving others in our wrong-doing:

- Setting a bad example for children, friends, or anyone who looks to us for guidance.

- Being preoccupied with selfish pursuits and totally unaware of the needs of others.

- Forgetting birthdays, holidays and other special occasions.

- Inflicting moral harm (e.g., sexual infidelity, broken promises, verbal abuse, lack of trust, lying).

Spiritual Wrongs: "Acts of omission" as a result of neglecting our obligations to God, to ourselves, to family and to community.

- Making no effort to fulfill our obligations and showing no gratitude toward others who have helped us.

- Avoiding self-development (e.g., health, education, recreation, creativity).

- Being inattentive to others in our lives by showing a lack of encouragement to them.

AMENDS LIST

Person	Relationship	My wrongdoing	Effect on Others	Effect on me
Joan	Wife	angry insults	fear, anger	guilt, shame
John	Co-worker	sexual advances at party	distrust, shame	loss of self-respect

AMENDS LIST EXERCISE

Select the person to whom you have caused the most harm and answer the following questions.

Name: _____ **Harm:** _____

- What is the reason for making the amend? _____
  _____
  _____
  _____

- What is your resistance to making the amend? _____
  _____
  _____
  _____

- How do you feel about making the amend? _____
  _____
  _____
  _____

- What character defects were demonstrated in your relationship with this person? _____
  _____
  _____
  _____

- Describe your willingness to ask for forgiveness and accept the consequences. _____
  _____
  _____
  _____

- When and how do you plan to make the amend? _____
  _____
  _____
  _____

STEP NINE

*Made direct amends to such people wherever possible,
except when to do so would injure them or others.*

*Therefore, if you are offering your gift at the altar and there
remember that your brother has something against you,
leave your gift there in front of the altar. First go and be
reconciled to your brother; then come and offer your gift.*
(Matthew 5:23-24)

Step Nine completes the forgiveness process that began in Step Four and fulfills our requirement to reconcile with others. In this Step, we clear our garden of the dead leaves and "rake up and discard" the old habits. We are ready to face our faults, to admit the degree of our wrongs, and to ask for and extend forgiveness. Accepting responsibility for the harm done can be an awkward experience, as it forces us to admit the affect we have had on others.

Since we began our recovery, we have come a long way toward developing a new lifestyle. We have seen how the powerlessness and unmanageability of our lives caused havoc. Our commitment to face our character defects, to admit them to others and, finally, to ask God for their removal has been a humbling experience. In Steps Eight and Nine, we proceed with the final stage of rebuilding our character.

Good judgment, a careful sense of timing, courage and stamina are the qualities we need to develop when working Step Nine. We will know we are ready to make amends when we are confident of our new skills and when others begin to observe that we are improving our lives. As we become more courageous, it will be easier and safer to talk honestly about our past behavior and admit to others that we have caused them harm.

Making amends will release us from many of the resentments of our past. It is a means of achieving serenity in our lives by seeking forgiveness from those whom we have harmed and making restitution where necessary. Without forgiveness, the resentments will continue to undermine our growth. Making amends releases us from guilt and promotes freedom and health in mind and body.

In preparing to make our amends, we realize that some people in our lives feel bitter toward us. They may feel threatened by us and resent our changed behavior. When considering the appropriateness of facing these people directly, we can pray about it and ask that Christ's wisdom be made known to us. If we are to forgive ourselves completely, we must first acknowledge the pain that others have endured as a result of our actions.

Some stumbling blocks appear in Step Nine. We may procrastinate by telling ourselves "the time is not yet right." We may delay by finding endless excuses to avoid facing those whom we have harmed. We must be honest with ourselves and not procrastinate because of fear. Fear is lack of courage, and courage is an important requirement for the successful completion of this Step, as well as the rest of the program. Our readiness to accept the consequences of our past and take responsibility for restoring the well-being of those whom we have harmed is the very spirit of Step Nine.

Another delaying tactic is the temptation to let bygones be bygones. We rationalize that our past is behind us, that there is no need to stir up more trouble. We fantasize that amends for past misdeeds are not necessary, that all we have to do is alter our current behavior. It is true that some of our past behaviors may be laid to rest without direct confrontation, but facing as many people and issues as possible is a good idea. The more situations we face, the more rapidly we will progress to our new life of peace and serenity.

Personal Reflection

In order to successfully complete Step Nine, we need to review our list from Step Eight and determine the appropriate way to make each amend. Most situations will require direct contact, although some may be handled by simply changing our behavior. Whichever alternative we choose, it is important that the process of making amends be as complete as possible.

● Who on your amends list causes you the most anxiety? What is your concern? _____

_____

_____

_____

1 JOHN 4:19-21
> We love because he first loved us. If anyone says, "I love God," yet hates his brother, he is a liar. For anyone who does not love his brother, whom he has seen, cannot love God, whom he has not seen.

● How does hatred for others interfere with your ability to love God? _____

_____

_____

_____

♦ ♦ ♦

Step Nine has two distinct parts regarding making amends:

"MADE DIRECT AMENDS TO SUCH PEOPLE WHEREVER POSSIBLE,"

People who are readily accessible and who can be approached as soon as we are ready.

These people include family members, creditors, co-workers and others to whom we owe an amend. They can be friends or enemies. As part of making the amend, we must try to repair the damage that has been done to the best of our ability. The other person's response may be surprising to us, especially if our amend is accepted—we may wonder why we waited so long to resolve the conflict.

● What is your reaction to the idea of making amends to your enemies? _____

_____

_____

_____

● What does making "direct amends" mean to you? _____

_____

_____

_____

MATTHEW 5:43-44

"You have heard that it was said, 'Love your neighbor and hate your enemy.' But I tell you: Love your enemies and pray for those who persecute you."

● Why is it important to love your enemies? _____

_____

_____

_____

◆ ◆ ◆

Situations that will not allow us to make direct personal contact.

This involves people who are no longer accessible or who are deceased. In these cases, indirect amends can satisfy our need for reconciliation and are accomplished through prayer or by writing a letter, as if we are actually communicating with the absent person. We can also make amends by performing a kindness for someone else we may not even know, but who is connected in some way to the person whom we have harmed.

● Describe how prayer or writing can help you to make amends where direct contact is not

possible. _____

_____

_____

_____

1 PETER 4:8-10

Above all, love each other deeply, because love covers over a multitude of sins. Offer hospitality to one another without grumbling. Each one should use whatever gift he has received to serve others, faithfully administering God's grace in its various forms.

● Give examples of occasions when you offered hospitality to another without grumbling.

_____

_____

_____

◆ ◆ ◆

"EXCEPT WHEN TO DO SO WOULD INJURE THEM OR OTHERS"

People to whom we can make only partial restitution because complete disclosure could cause harm to them or others.

These people may include spouses, ex-partners, former business associates or friends. We must analyze the harm they would suffer if complete disclosure was made. This is especially true in cases of infidelity. In such situations, irreparable damage could occur to all parties.

Even if the matter must be discussed, we should avoid bringing harm to third parties. Amends for infidelity can be made by concentrating sincere affection and attention on persons to whom we have made loving commitments.

- Who on your amends list falls into this category? How will complete disclosure cause harm? _____

_____

_____

_____

MATTHEW 5:23-24

"Therefore, if you are offering your gift at the altar and there remember that your brother has something against you, leave your gift there in front of the altar. First go and be reconciled to your brother; then come and offer your gift.

- List any difficulties you are having in making amends to those who continue to hold something against you. _____

_____

_____

_____

◆ ◆ ◆

In cases involving serious consequences, such as potential loss of employment, imprisonment or other harm to one's family, we need to weigh the options carefully. We should not be deterred from making amends through fear of incurring injury to ourselves, but only through the possibility of causing injury to others. If we choose to delay merely out of fear for ourselves, we will be the ones to suffer. We will delay our growth and experience regression in our progress toward building a new life.

- Cite a situation in which direct amends could have serious consequences. Explain. _____

_____

_____

_____

EZEKIEL 33:15-16

...if he gives back what he took in pledge for a loan, returns what he has stolen, follows the decrees that give life, and does no evil, he will surely live; he will not die. None of the sins he has committed will be remembered against him. He has done what is just and right; he will surely live.

- How can giving back what you have taken be seen as making an amend? _____

_____

_____

_____

◆ ◆ ◆

Situations which require deferred action.

In these areas, seeking additional counsel is helpful in assessing our judgment of the situation. Abruptly approaching an individual who still suffers deeply from the injustices we have done is seldom wise. In situations where our own pain is still deeply imbedded, patience might be the wise choice. Timing is important to gaining and growing from the experience and in preventing further injury.

- Who on your amends list falls into this category? What harm can be caused by making an amend? _____

  _____

  _____

1 THESSALONIANS 5:11
  Therefore encourage one another and build each other up, just as in fact you are doing.

- How can encouraging another person help you in preparing to make an amend for a wrongdoing? _____

  _____

  _____

ROMANS 14:13
  Therefore let us stop passing judgment on one another. Instead, make up your mind not to put any stumbling block or obstacle in your brother's way.

- How has passing judgment on others caused them harm? _____

  _____

  _____

  _____

♦ ♦ ♦

As we have learned, certain situations require special consideration. It is better to proceed slowly and succeed with the amend, rather than hurry and cause more damage. Here, God can be a great source of aid and comfort. He has gotten us this far, and we need to be constantly aware that our progress is greatly influenced by His presence with us now.

- Cite instances in which being impatient to make an amend proved harmful. _____

  _____

  _____

  _____

LUKE 6:35-36
  "But love your enemies, do good to them, and lend to them without expecting to get anything back. Then your reward will be great, and you will be sons of the Most High, because he is kind to the ungrateful and wicked."

- What rewards do you expect to receive if you are generous with others? _____
_____
_____
_____

◆ ◆ ◆

To facilitate making the amend, prepare a schedule listing the persons to contact, what you will say, how you will say it and when you will say it. Writing letters and making phone calls are acceptable ways of making amends if face-to-face contact is not possible. In some cases, meeting in person may not be the most desirable approach. The important thing is to initiate reconciliation before it is too late. Successful amends-making will produce improved relationships with those whom we have harmed and promote positive interactions with new acquaintances. Our new ways of relating will empower us to achieve and maintain healthy relationships.

- How has making amends improved your relationships with others? _____
_____
_____
_____

ROMANS 13:8
Let no debt remain outstanding, except the continuing debt to love one another, for he who loves his fellowman has fulfilled the law.

- List any outstanding debts you have that need to be repaid. How do you plan to make
restitution? _____
_____
_____
_____

◆ ◆ ◆

When working this Step, we need to distinguish between amends and apologies. Though apologies are sometimes appropriate, they are not substitutes for making amends. A person can apologize for being late for work, but until the behavior is corrected, an amend cannot be made. It is important to apologize when necessary, but it is more important to commit to changing the unacceptable behavior.

- How do you distinguish between apologies and amends? _____
_____
_____
_____

- List an example in which you apologized, but did not make an amend. _____
_____
_____
_____

ROMANS 12:17-18

Do not repay anyone evil for evil. Be careful to do what is right in the eyes of everybody. If it is possible, as far as it depends on you, live at peace with everyone.

● How are you damaged when you seek revenge instead of living at peace wherever possible? _____

_____

_____

_____

◆ ◆ ◆

Occasional emotional or spiritual relapses are to be expected and should be dealt with promptly. If not, they will block our ability to make successful amends. When these relapses occur, we must accept them as signals that we are not working the Program effectively. Perhaps we have turned away from God and need to return to Step Three; or we may have eliminated something from our inventory and must return to Step Four; or we may be unwilling to relinquish a character defect and need to return to Step Six.

● List examples of recent relapses and how you dealt with them. _____

_____

_____

_____

● Which character defects caused the relapses? _____

_____

_____

_____

PHILIPPIANS 2:3-4

Do nothing out of selfish ambition or vain conceit, but in humility consider others better than yourselves. Each of you should look not only to your own interests, but also to the interests of others.

● In which areas of your life are you still being selfish? _____

_____

_____

_____

◆ ◆ ◆

Steps Eight and Nine help us bury the past. Through these Steps, we reconcile ourselves to taking responsibility for causing injury to others and for making restitution where necessary. We have a chance to redeem ourselves for past misdeeds by making amends and can look forward to a healthy and rewarding future life. We are now able to rebuild our self-esteem, achieve peaceful relations with ourselves and others, and live in harmony with our own personal world and with God.

- How will completing Step Nine enable you to bury the past and improve your self-esteem? _____

  _____

  _____

  _____

- What difficulties are you having in making direct amends? _____

  _____

  _____

  _____

COLOSSIANS 3:12-13

Therefore, as God's chosen people, holy and dearly loved, clothe yourselves with compassion, kindness, humility, gentleness and patience. Bear with each other and forgive whatever grievances you may have against one another. Forgive as the Lord forgave you.

- How does compassion, kindness and patience contribute to the serenity in your life?

  _____

  _____

  _____

◆ ◆ ◆

AMENDS TO OTHERS EXERCISE

The following is a summary of ideas and procedures that have been useful in preparing for and making the amends required in Step Nine.

Attitude

- Being willing to love and forgive yourself and the person to whom an amend is to be made.

- Knowing what you want to say and being careful not to blame the person with whom you are communicating.

- Taking responsibility for what you are going to say.

- Being willing to accept the consequences.

- Resisting the desire for a specific response from the other person.

- Being willing to turn your anxieties over to God.

Preparation

- Devoting time to prayer and meditation.

- Delaying the amend if you are angry or upset and doing more Step Four inventory work.

- Keeping it simple. Details and explanations aren't necessary.

- Remembering that the amend does not focus on the other person's part in the situation.

- Expressing your desire or asking permission to make the amend. For example: *I am involved in a program that requires me to be aware of the harm I have done to others and to take responsibility for my actions. I'd like to make amends to you. Are you willing to receive them?*

Sample Amends

- *I was (scared, overwhelmed, feeling abandoned, etc.) when _____ happened between us. I ask your forgiveness for (harm done) and for anything else I may have done in the past by my thoughts, words or actions that caused you pain. I didn't mean to cause you pain. I ask your forgiveness and assure you of my intention to extend goodwill to you.*

- *I want to make an amend to you about _____ . For all those words that were said out of (fear, thoughtlessness, etc.) and confusion, I ask your forgiveness. I extend my promise of love and caring toward you.*

Select a person to whom you wish to make an amend.

- Who is the person and what is the reason for the amend? _____

  _____

  _____

  _____

- How will you communicate the amend? _____

  _____

  _____

  _____

AMENDS TO SELF EXERCISE

The following are some guidelines to use when making amends to yourself.

Attitude

- Being willing to love and forgive yourself.
- Knowing what you want to say and taking responsibility for your actions.
- Having reasonable expectations of yourself.
- Being willing to turn your anxieties over to God.

Preparation

- Devoting time to prayer and meditation.
- Delaying the amend if you are angry or upset and doing more Step Four inventory work.
- Keeping it simple. Explanations are not necessary.
- Remembering the amend is to yourself and does not pertain to others.

Sample Amends

- *I was (scared, overwhelmed, feeling abandoned, etc.) when _____ happened. I forgive myself for the (harm done) and anything else I may have done in the past by my thoughts, words or actions that may have caused me harm.*
- *I want to make an amend to myself about _____ . I forgive myself for all the words that I said out of (fear, thoughtlessness, etc.) and confusion.*

Write an amends letter to yourself.

- Dear _____ ,

  _____

  _____

  _____

  _____

  _____

  _____

  _____

  _____

  _____

  _____

- How do you feel as a result of writing this letter? _____

  _____

  _____

  _____

STEP TEN

*Continued to take personal inventory and, when
we were wrong, promptly admitted it.*

*So, if you think you are standing firm, be
careful that you don't fall.*
(1 Corinthians 10:12)

In Step Ten, we begin the maintenance segment of the Steps. We will learn how to sustain what we have accomplished, become more confident and proceed with joy along our spiritual journey. The first nine Steps put our house in order and enabled us to change some of our destructive behavior patterns. By continuing our work on the Steps, we will increase our capacity to develop new and healthier ways of taking care of ourselves and relating to others.

As we begin to experience some peace and serenity in our lives, some of us may wonder if it is permanent or just temporary. Working the Steps has helped us to see how fragile and vulnerable we are. With daily practice of the Steps, and with Christ's loving presence in our lives, we will be able to achieve and maintain our newfound equilibrium. Our relating skills will improve, and we will see how our interaction with others assumes a new quality.

At this point, we may be tempted to revert to our old bravado and believe we are healed. We may think we have all the answers and can stop here. We feel comfortable with ourselves and see no need to continue with the Program. We allow other activities to interfere and find excuses for skipping meetings and abandoning the Program. We must resist this temptation to quit and realize that giving in will deprive us of realizing the goal we have set for ourselves. We must recognize that the successes we have experienced can be maintained only if we are willing to practice the Program daily for the rest of our lives.

Step Ten points the way toward continued spiritual growth. In the past, we were constantly burdened by the results of our inattention to what we were doing. We allowed small problems to become large by ignoring them until they multiplied. Through our lack of sensitivity and skills to improve our behavior, we allowed our character defects to create havoc in our lives. In Step Ten, we consciously examine our daily conduct and make adjustments where necessary. We look at ourselves, see our errors, promptly admit them and make corrections.

While we are working so carefully to monitor our actions and reactions, we must not judge ourselves too harshly. We need to recognize that nurturing ourselves emotionally and spiritually requires daily vigilance, loving understanding and patience. Life is never static; it is constantly changing, and each change requires adjustment and growth.

A personal inventory is a daily examination of our strengths and weaknesses, motives and behaviors. It is as important as prayer in nurturing our spiritual development. Taking inventory is not a time-consuming task and can usually be accomplished in fifteen minutes per day. When done with discipline and regularity, this is a small price to pay for continuing the good work we have begun.

We need to monitor signs of attempting to manage our lives alone or slipping into past patterns such as resentment, dishonesty or selfishness. When we see these temptations arising, we must immediately ask God to forgive us and make amends. Daily practice of Step Ten maintains our honesty and humility and allows us to continue our development.

Taking regular inventory makes us more conscious of our strengths and weaknesses. We are less inclined to yield to feelings of anger, loneliness and self-righteousness if we remain emotionally balanced and gather courage as we see our strengths increasing. Our personal inventory helps us discover who we are, what we are and where we are going. We become more focused and capable of living the Christian life we desire.

Personal Reflection

The Program's emphasis on daily inventory is based on the realization that many of us haven't developed the necessary tools for self-appraisal. As we become familiar and comfortable with personal inventories, we will be willing to invest the time required in exchange for the rewards received. Three types of inventories are recommended; each serves a different purpose. These are **Spot-Check Inventory, Daily Inventory** and **Long-Term Periodic Inventory.**

- How will daily inventory help you develop the ability to appraise your behavior? _____

_____

_____

_____

PSALM 34:12
Whoever of you loves life and desires to see many good days, keep your tongue from evil and your lips from speaking lies. Turn from evil and do good; seek peace and pursue it.

- How does working the Twelve Steps help you turn from evil and seek peace? _____

_____

_____

_____

◆ ◆ ◆

Spot-Check Inventory

Spot-checking is stopping for a few moments several times each day to analyze what is happening. It is a short review of our actions, thoughts and motives and can be useful in calming stormy emotions. It is a tool for examining each situation, seeing where we are wrong and taking prompt corrective action. Taking frequent inventories and immediately admitting our wrongs keeps us free from guilt and supports our spiritual growth.

- Describe a recent situation in which you were wrong and promptly admitted it. _____

_____

_____

_____

- How does taking a daily inventory support your spiritual growth? _____

_____

_____

_____

ROMANS 12:13

For by the grace given me I say to every one of you: Do not think of yourself more highly than you ought, but rather think of yourself with sober judgment, in accordance with the measure of faith God has given you.

- What is your current opinion of yourself and your progress in the Program? _____

_____

_____

_____

♦ ♦ ♦

Daily Inventory (See page 129)

It is important to stop at the end of each day, review what has happened and examine our involvement to remind us that this is a daily program, lived one day at a time. It keeps us focused on the present and prevents us from worrying about the future or living in the past.

- How does daily inventory improve your ability to get along with others? _____

_____

_____

_____

MATTHEW 5:25-26

"Settle matters quickly with your adversary who is taking you to court. Do it while you are still with him on the way, or he may hand you over to the judge, and the judge may hand you over to the officer, and you may be thrown into prison. I tell you the truth, you will not get out until you have paid the last penny."

- Cite an example in which correcting your wrongs saved you from unnecessary conse-

quences and pain. _____

_____

_____

_____

♦ ♦ ♦

The daily inventory can be viewed as a balance sheet for the day—a summary of the good as well as the bad. It is an opportunity to reflect on our interaction with other people. In the situations where we did well, we can feel good and acknowledge progress. In those situations where we tried and failed, we need to acknowledge our attempt; for, in fact, we did try. Our failures can illuminate our errors; we can then make amends and move forward with a quiet mind. As we work the Program, we can be assured that our number of successes will continue to increase.

- List examples of recent behavior that indicate you are successfully learning new ways of relating to others. _____

  _____

  _____

  _____

- Cite a recent situation in which you did not behave appropriately. What did you do when you realized you were in error? _____

  _____

  _____

  _____

EPHESIANS 4:25-28

> *Therefore each of you must put off falsehood and speak truthfully to his neighbor, for we are all members of one body. "In your anger do not sin": Do not let the sun go down while you are still angry, and do not give the devil a foothold. He who has been stealing must steal no longer, but must work, doing something useful with his own hands, that he may have something to share with those in need.*

- Describe a recent situation in which you did not resolve angry feelings. What effect did it have on you? _____

  _____

  _____

◆ ◆ ◆

Future situations may arise that will challenge our integrity and commitment. We need to be as honest and clear about our intentions as possible. Things to consider are:

- If we are slipping back, trying to control and manipulate others, we need to recognize this and ask God to correct it.

- If we are comparing ourselves to others and feeling inferior, we need to reach out to supportive friends and examine our feelings, in order to renew our own sense of self-acceptance.

- If we are becoming obsessive or compulsive and not taking care of ourselves, we need to stop and ask our Higher Power for help, not only in determining the unmet needs we are trying to fulfill, but also how to meet these needs.

- If we are fearing authority figures, we need to find the reason for our fear, acknowledge it, and ask our Higher Power for help in reacting appropriately.

- If we are depressed, we need to discover the central issue that is causing us to feel withdrawn or sorry for ourselves.

- If we are withholding our feelings, being uncommunicative or giving in to others' wants and needs, we need to take the necessary risks and express our feelings assertively.

- Which ineffective behaviors are most consistently present when taking your daily inventory? _____

  _____

  _____

- What is your resistance to having these defects removed? _____
  _____
  _____
  _____

JAMES 1:23-25
Anyone who listens to the word but does not do what it says is like a man who looks at his face in a mirror and, after looking at himself, goes away and immediately forgets what he looks like. But the man who looks intently into the perfect law that gives freedom, and continues to do this, not forgetting what he has heard, but doing it—he will be blessed in what he does.

- How has this Program enabled you to look at yourself in the mirror and accept who you
  are? _____
  _____
  _____
  _____

◆ ◆ ◆

Long-Term Periodic Inventory

A long-term periodic inventory can be accomplished by being alone or going away for a period of time. These are special days that can be set aside for reflecting on our lives by attending a retreat or simply being in solitude. This is an important time and provides an opportunity for us to renew our intention to live a new life in Christ.

- How much time do you spend alone reflecting on your life? How is it helpful in your
  recovery? _____
  _____
  _____
  _____

2 CORINTHIANS 5:17
Therefore, if anyone is in Christ, he is a new creation; the old has gone, the new has come!

- How has your renewed relationship with Christ helped you to become a new creation?
  _____
  _____
  _____

◆ ◆ ◆

This inventory can be done once or twice a year and will give us a chance to reflect on our progress from a clearer perspective. We will have an opportunity to see the remarkable changes we have made and to renew our hope and courage. We must be careful not to inflate our ego and must remind ourselves that our progress is a product of God's help and our careful spiritual growth. Long-term inventories help us to recognize problem areas and enable us to make the necessary corrections promptly. As a result of our new experiences, we sometimes find new defects as well as new strengths.

- What new defects have emerged as a result of your new experiences? _____

  _____

  _____

  _____

- What new strengths have emerged as a result of your new experiences? _____

  _____

  _____

  _____

EPHESIANS 4:22-24

You were taught, with regard to your former way of life, to put off your old self, which is being corrupted by its deceitful desires; to be made new in the attitude of your minds; and to put on the new self, created to be like God in true righteousness and holiness.

- How do you view your new image as being more focused on what God wants for you,

  rather than what you want? _____

  _____

  _____

  _____

◆ ◆ ◆

If we sincerely desire to change our way of life, take personal inventory on a regular basis and pay attention to the sharing of other recovering friends, we will discover that we are not unique. All people get upset occasionally and are not always "right." Through this awareness, we develop the ability to be forgiving and understanding and to love others for who they are. By being kind, courteous and fair, we will often receive the same in return and can expect to achieve harmony in many of our relationships. As we progress in our recovery, we see how pointless it is to become angry or to allow others to inflict emotional pain on us. Taking periodic, regular inventory and promptly admitting our wrongs keeps us from harboring resentments and allows us to maintain our dignity and respect for ourselves and others.

- How is daily inventory helping you remain free of resentments and allowing you to deal

  with issues promptly? _____

  _____

  _____

  _____

PROVERBS 14:29-30

A patient man has great understanding, but a quick-tempered man displays folly. A heart at peace gives life to the body, but envy rots the bones.

- List examples where you have been understanding. Describe the feelings that resulted from maintaining your composure. _____

_____

_____

_____

♦ ♦ ♦

The conscientious practice of Step Ten has many benefits; most importantly, it strengthens and protects our recovery. We find additional rewards in many areas, such as:

- When old behaviors reappear, they are simply repetitions of learned patterns of behavior. They reflect choices of our unconscious mind as it defended us against feelings of pain, strife, helplessness, guilt, revenge, disapproval, etc. Clinging to these patterns keeps us from achieving the spiritual growth we so desire.

- We feel safe when something is familiar to us, even though it is a negative behavior pattern or addiction from the past that may ultimately cause us pain. We use it anyway, because it is familiar to us.

- We victimize ourselves by allowing the past to occupy our thoughts. We can let go of the past by acknowledging the unmet responsibilities that created our struggle.

- Releasing an old behavior pattern can be frightening. By surrendering it to our Higher Power, we learn to trust that we will receive the needed support to develop behaviors that are more appropriate for our present wants and needs.

- We can reach out to loving and supportive friends. They are important ingredients in our recovery.

- How do you deal with old behaviors when they reappear? _____

_____

_____

_____

- In what areas are you slipping back into old behavior patterns? _____

_____

_____

_____

1 CORINTHIANS 10:12
   So, if you think you are standing firm, be careful that you don't fall.

- What precaution are you taking to prevent becoming overly confident and falling into past behavior patterns? _____

_____

_____

_____

♦ ♦ ♦

Successful working of Step Ten enables us to be genuinely sorry for our wrongs. It assists us in continually striving for improvement in our relationships with others. Learning to face our faults on a daily basis and correcting them promptly is the formula for improving our character and lifestyle. Delay in admitting our wrongs indicates a resistance to practicing Step Ten. This is harmful and will only make matters worse. The ongoing practice of Step Ten has many benefits; most importantly, it strengthens and maintains our recovery. We find additional rewards in many areas, such as:

- Relationship problems diminish. Taking inventory and admitting our wrongs promptly dissolves many misunderstandings without further incident.

- We learn to express ourselves, rather than fear being "found out." We see that, by being honest, we do not need to hide behind a false front.

- We no longer have to pretend we are flawless and, thus, can be candid about admitting our wrongs.

- Through admitting our own wrongs, others may, in turn, become aware of the ineffectiveness of their own behavior. We develop a true understanding of others and become capable of intimacy.

● What success are you having in taking daily inventory, seeing your faults, and promptly admitting them? _____

_____

_____

_____

● How are your new habits supporting your recovery? _____

_____

_____

_____

EPHESIANS 5:15-16
Be very careful, then, how you live—not as unwise but as wise, making the most of every opportunity, because the days are evil.

● Describe the changes you have made in your lifestyle. _____

_____

_____

_____

◆ ◆ ◆

STEP TEN DAILY INVENTORY LOG

Using the following ratings, record your level of functioning each day:

0 = Poor   1 = Fair   2 = Average   3 = Good   4 = Excellent

Characteristic (Weakness)	Mon.	Tue.	Wed.	Thur.	Fri.	Sat.	Sun.
Anger/Resentment							
Approval seeking							
Caretaking							
Control							
Denial							
Depression/Self-pity							
Dishonesty							
Frozen feelings							
Isolation							
Jealousy							
Perfectionism							
Procrastination							
Worry (past or future)							

Characteristic (Strength)	Mon.	Tues.	Wed.	Thur.	Fri.	Sat.	Sun.
Forgiveness							
Generosity							
Honesty							
Humility							
Patience							
Risk-taking							
Self-nurturing							
Tolerance							
Trust							

● What were your experiences in completing this exercise? _____

_____

_____

_____

● How did it help you be more aware of your behavior? _____

_____

_____

_____

Notes: _____

_____

_____

_____

_____

_____

_____

_____

_____

_____

_____

_____

_____

_____

_____

_____

_____

_____

_____

_____

_____

_____

_____

_____

_____

_____

_____

_____

_____

_____

_____

_____

_____

_____

_____

_____

STEP ELEVEN

*Sought through prayer and meditation to improve our
conscious contact with God as we understood Him,
praying only for knowledge of His will for us
and the power to carry that out.*

Let the word of Christ dwell in you richly.
(Colossians 3:16a)

As we begin our work in Step Eleven, we clearly see that Steps Ten and Eleven are the tools which will help us sustain the progress we have made in Steps One through Nine. In the first three Steps, we began to understand the seriousness of our condition and established the foundation for dealing with our problems. In Steps Four through Nine, we experienced a process similar to that of taking our car to the garage for a long-overdue, major overhaul. We devoted the time and energy required to make the necessary repairs and restore our "engine" to its proper running condition. In Steps Ten and Eleven, we have the opportunity to keep ourselves in tune by devoting time to regular service and maintenance. We learn to recognize problems, to correct them promptly, and to continually look for ways to improve our new skills for living life to the fullest. To the degree that we are willing to provide the required maintenance, we will find that our lives will run smoothly.

Prior to Step Eleven, we made contact with God in three of the Steps. In Step Three, we made a decision to turn our wills and our lives over to His care; in Step Five, we admitted our wrongs to Him; in Step Seven, we humbly asked Him to remove our shortcomings. In Step Eleven, we use prayer and meditation to improve our conscious contact with God, as well as become sensitive and responsive to His guidance. To continue our spiritual growth, we must repeat these Steps regularly.

Through the progress we have made in working the Steps, we are learning more about what we want to achieve in the Program. To protect what we have learned, we must continually seek to know God's will for us. A daily regimen of prayer and meditation makes it clear that relief from pain of the past is just a day-to-day reprieve—we must relentlessly pursue recovery on a daily basis. Those of us who have experienced the hell and chaos caused by our willful acts realize that we worshipped false gods such as drugs, sex, or money, and were often participants in addictive relationships. For us, surrendering to the Twelve Steps was not the step that led us to heaven, but was, in fact, the step that led us out of the hell that our lives had become.

Spiritual growth and development occur slowly and only through discipline. The best example of the discipline of prayer is that of Jesus as He prayed frequently to know His Father's will. In the Lord's Prayer, the singularly most important element is "Thy will be done, on earth as it is in heaven." This may be interpreted as "May your will be realized throughout all of space, time and creation. God, if it is to be done, it is for you to bring it about." As our self-esteem increases and Jesus Christ, our Higher Power becomes a trusted friend, we grow more confident that He is even present with us when we pray.

131

Meditation is an important way of seeking God's will for us, of setting aside our own intentions and receiving God's guidance. Meditating can quiet our minds and remove the barriers of our conscious thoughts. When properly done, this process will calm us emotionally and relax us physically. We will the release energy we normally expend keeping our emotions in high gear and our bodies tense with anxiety.

Our approach to Step Eleven will vary in intent and intensity; it indicates our commitment to a prayerful life. If we are communing and are communicating with God, His joy will infuse our fellowship and friendship with others. We will reap rich benefits. Ideally, we practice this Step daily upon awakening and retiring, to remind us that we must sincerely and humbly want God's will for us.

NOTE: Before proceeding, refer to **Guidelines for Prayer and Meditating on God's Word** on page 138.

Personal Reflection

Praying only for knowledge of God's will for us and the power to carry it out helps us set aside our self-serving motives and interact well with others. We receive reassurance of God's presence and know that His will is for us to be restored to health. Scripture gives examples of how we will behave when we allow God's will to work through us. In Luke 6:35-38, we are told: "Love your enemies, do good to them, and lend to them...be merciful...do not judge...do not condemn...forgive...give..." When we follow Luke' teachings we feel peaceful and serene.

- How can the principles of Step Eleven help you interact better with others? _____

_____

_____

_____

- How does prayer help you get in touch with God and open your heart to knowing His will? _____

_____

_____

_____

LUKE 6:45

"The good man brings good things out of the good stored up in his heart. For out of the outflow of his heart his mouth speaks."

- In what way has this Program helped you to see good things about yourself? _____

_____

_____

MARK 11:24

"Therefore I tell you, whatever you ask for in prayer, believe that you have received it, and it will be yours. And when you stand praying, if you hold anything against anyone, forgive him, so that your Father in heaven may forgive you your sins."

● Describe how your belief in prayer has supported you in asking to know God's will for you? _____

_____

_____

_____

◆ ◆ ◆

Spending time meditating on God's word enables us to become better acquainted with God in the same way that we become acquainted with someone we would really like to know; that is, by spending time with Him. Meditation can be difficult in the beginning. We are accustomed to being active and may feel uncomfortable with sitting still and calming our busy thoughts. We may feel we are wasting time, instead of doing something more productive. Actually, for us, nothing could be more productive.

● What is your experience of meditation? _____

_____

_____

_____

HOSEA 6:3

"Let us acknowledge the LORD; let us press on to acknowledge him. As surely as the sun rises, he will appear; he will come to us like the winter rains, like the spring rains that water the earth."

● Describe the difficulties you have in allowing God to come into your life. _____

_____

_____

_____

◆ ◆ ◆

In the act of meditating, we recall, ponder and apply our knowledge of God's ways, purposes and promises. It is an activity of holy thought, consciously performed in the presence of God, under the eye of God and by the help of God, as a two-way communion with Him. Its purpose is to clear our mental and spiritual vision and let His truth make its full and proper impact on our minds and hearts. Meditation humbles us as we contemplate God's greatness and glory and allow His Spirit to encourage, reassure and comfort us.

● How does meditating improve your conscious contact with God? _____

_____

_____

_____

MATTHEW 6:6

"But when you pray, go into your room, close the door and pray to your Father, who is unseen. Then your Father, who sees what is done in secret, will reward you."

- What do you experience when quietly praying to God? Describe any feelings of discomfort you have in doing this. _____

  _____

  _____

  _____

PSALM 25:4-5

"Show me your ways, O LORD, teach me your paths; guide me in your truth and teach me, for you are God my Savior, and my hope is in you all day long."

- Cite a situation in which God showed you the correct path to follow. _____

  _____

  _____

  _____

♦ ♦ ♦

In developing a routine for prayer and meditation, we seek times and places to receive God's presence and be available for Him. Some simple guidelines for learning to pray and meditate are:

- Pray and meditate in solitude. Be alone and undisturbed, so you can be totally free from distractions.

- Pray and meditate in silence, or talk quietly to God without interruptions. Outside influences disrupt your concentration and inhibit your ability to tell God your thoughts and feelings.

- Set aside quality time. Do not wait until you are tired or your ability to clear you mind is hindered.

- Listen carefully. God has messages for you, just as you have messages for Him.

- Review your daily inventory with God. Admit your wrongs, ask for forgiveness and make amends to Him as needed.

- End your session by asking for knowledge of His will and the power to carry it out.

- What is your current routine of prayer? How can you improve it? _____

  _____

  _____

  _____

- What is your current routine of meditation? How can you improve it? _____

  _____

  _____

  _____

MATTHEW 7:7

"Ask and it will be given to you; seek and you will find; knock and the door will be opened to you."

- List a current request you have made of God. How does this request indicate that you are seeking God's will rather than your own? _____

_____

_____

_____

◆ ◆ ◆

If we are progressing satisfactorily with Step Eleven by praying and meditating daily, we will see signs along the way. We will feel more at peace in our daily affairs, and will experience deep gratitude for the ongoing healing of disabled behavior. We will feel as though we have finally achieved a rightful place in the world. Feelings of self-worth will replace feelings of shame. These signs tell us that God is guiding and sustaining our recovery.

- What events in your life indicate that you are successfully practicing Step Eleven? _____

_____

_____

_____

PSALM 1:1-3

"Blessed is the man who does not walk in the counsel of the wicked or stand in the way of sinners or sit in the seat of mockers. But his delight is in the law of the Lord, and on his law he meditates day and night. He is like a tree planted by streams of water, which yields its fruit in season and whose leaf does not wither. Whatever it does prospers."

- What events indicate that you are conforming to God's law, rather than to your own idea of what is right. _____

_____

_____

_____

◆ ◆ ◆

Combining prayer and meditating on God's word with self-examination is the secret to successfully working the Steps and moving toward a rewarding spiritual life. No matter how dedicated we are to recovery, we all have moments of doubt about the direction of our lives. We may even question the need to continue working the Steps. Sometimes, we are tempted to regress to our old compulsive behavior. We tend to be especially vulnerable when we feel pressured for accomplishment and expect events to follow our own time schedule. In our frustration, we seize control from God's hands and attempt to hasten the process through our own willfullness. When we do this, we are not following God's guidance and must renew the commitment we made in Step Three.

- Describe any doubts you may have about the direction your life is taking? _____

_____

_____

_____

- Cite a recent situation in which you were under pressure and took control away from God. _____

_____

_____

_____

PSALM 119:105-106

"Your word is a lamp to my feet and a light for my path. I have taken an oath and confirmed it, that I will follow your righteous laws."

- What is your current commitment to God as it relates to your desire to do His will? ____

_____

_____

_____

◆ ◆ ◆

Our power to implement God's will can be challenged in those moments when our lives seem to be crumbling. Again, the best example of faithfulness is the way in which Jesus persevered during the challenges of His experiences toward the end of His life on earth. The strength of His faith can be summarized by this prayer, made in Gethsemane as He was overwhelmed by what lay before Him: "…My Father, if it is possible, may this cup be taken from me. Yet not as I will, but as you will." (Matthew 26:39) During stressful moments, reflecting on Steps Three and Eleven will help us maintain our peace and serenity.

- How does your faith in Christ help you carry out God's will for you? _____

_____

_____

_____

PHILIPPIANS 4:6

"Do not be anxious about anything, but in everything, by prayer and petition, with thanksgiving, present your requests to God."

- How does your communication with God reduce your anxieties? _____

_____

_____

_____

◆ ◆ ◆

Praying and meditating give us an opportunity to seek God's plan for us. He gave us intellect and free will, through which we think and act. As part of successfully practicing Step Eleven, we must not create excuses to delay our actions, rationalizing that we are "waiting" for God's will. Part of doing God's will is taking action, trusting that God's Holy Spirit is working through us. In unclear situations, it is sometimes wise to seek outside counsel. Revelations may come to us through other people or new experiences, as God continues to reach out to us in different ways. After careful review of the situation, our guidance may be clear and compelling or still unclear. If unclear, we must be patient—more will be revealed to us. If we cannot wait, we must select the best course of action and trust that God is with us, guiding us as we go. Our faith in His guidance will allow us to receive what needs to be revealed to us. The way we feel and function clearly indicates if God's will is being done.

● Describe a recent situation in which you delayed taking action because you were "waiting" for God's will? What were the consequences? _____

_____

_____

_____

MATTHEW 21:22

"If you believe, you will receive whatever you ask for in prayer."

● Cite an example in which God answered your prayers through another individual or a new experience. _____

_____

_____

_____

LUKE 6:49

"But the one who hears my words and does not put them into practice is like a man who built a house on the ground without a foundation. The moment the torrent struck that house, it collapsed and its destruction was complete."

● List an example of doubting God. What were the consequences of your doubts? _____

_____

_____

_____

◆ ◆ ◆

Our earthly walk with God, as exemplified by Jesus Christ, is designed to bring us a life that is filled with abundance. This is God's will for us as described in the teachings of Jesus. If we will "...in everything, do to others what you would have them do to you..." (Matthew 7:12), our daily lives will exemplify what Step Eleven means.

● What is your opinion of your life today? How has the quality of your life improved as a result of your working the Steps? _____

_____

_____

_____

ISAIAH 30:21

"Whether you turn to the right or to the left, your ears will hear a voice behind you, saying, "This is the way; walk in it.""

● Cite an example of God's way for you at this time in your life. _____
_____
_____
_____

GUIDELINES FOR PRAYER AND MEDITATING ON GOD'S WORD

An overview of prayer and meditation for a given day may be outlined as follows:

At the beginning of the day, review your plans and:

- Ask God for direction in your thoughts and actions.
  - To keep you free from self-pity, dishonesty or selfishness.
  - To provide the guidance needed to take care of any problems.
- Ask God for freedom from self-will.
  - To prevent making requests unless others will be helped.
  - To avoid praying for our own selfish needs.

During the day, in moments of indecision or fear:

- Ask God for inspiration and guidance.
- Reflect on Step Three and turn it over.
  - Relax and breathe deeply several times.
  - Be aware of any desire to struggle with a situation or person.
- Pray to God as often as necessary during the day.
  - *God, please remove this* _____ *(feeling, obsession, addiction, etc.)*
  - *Lord, not my will, but Thine be done.*
- If possible, call a support person to identify and share what is happening.

At the end of the day, review the events that happened and:

- Reflect on Step Ten and take a personal inventory.
  - Ask God for guidance in taking corrective action.
- Ask God for knowledge of His will for you.
- Ask God's forgiveness where needed, and acknowledge that this review is not intended to cause obsessive thinking, worry, remorse, or morbid reflection.
- Give thanks to God for the guidance and blessings that were part of the day.

STEP TWELVE

Having had a spiritual awakening as the result of these Steps,
we tried to carry this message to others, and to practice
these principles in all our affairs.

Brothers, if someone is caught in a sin, you who
are spiritual should restore him gently. But
watch yourself, or you also may be tempted.

(Galatians 6:1)

The Twelfth Step completes the climb of this particular mountain. Remembering the milestones in this adventure brings to mind the pain and joy we have experienced while accomplishing our objective. Our experiences have been unique and individual to each of us. We now realize that all the events of our lives have pulled together to show us our connection to God and creation. Our spiritual awakening has changed us, so now we have the capacity to live our lives as an expression of God's will. An example of this type of transformation is beautifully captured in Titus 3:3-7:

> *"At one time we too were foolish, disobedient, deceived and enslaved by all kinds of passions and pleasures. We lived in malice and envy, being hated and hating one another. But when the kindness and love of God our Savior appeared, he saved us, not because of righteous things we had done, but because of His mercy. He saved us through the washing of rebirth and renewal by the Holy Spirit, whom he poured out on us generously through Jesus Christ our Savior, so that, having been justified by His grace, we might become heirs having the hope of eternal life."*

Step Twelve requires that we be instrumental in helping others receive the message of The Twelve Steps. Many of us were introduced to this Program by someone who was working the Twelfth Step. Now we have the opportunity to promote our own growth by helping others. Our willingness to share our commitment to recovery and our growing awareness of God's presence in our lives keep us ever-vigilant for ways to share our new confidence. This program calls us to take responsibility for the daily living out of our values. The Apostle Paul clearly instructed us in this action by saying: "But in your hearts set apart Christ as Lord. Always be prepared to give an answer to everyone who asks you to give the reason for the hope that you have. But do this with gentleness and respect..."(1 Peter 3:15)

This Step reminds us that we have not yet completed our journey to wholeness. To continue our process of growth, we must be aware that we have just begun to learn the principles that will enhance our walk with the Lord. Each of the Twelve Steps is a vital part of fulfilling God's plan for us. When our daily challenges distract us and separate us from God, we can use the Steps as tools for coping with our problems. Step One reminds us of our powerlessness; Steps Two and Three show us the ongoing need for God's help; Steps Four through Nine guide us through self-examination and amends-making; Steps Ten and Eleven help us minimize our slips and keep in touch with God. Conscientious attention to working the Steps develops in us a level of love, acceptance, honesty, selflessness and peace of mind unequalled at any other time in our lives. The hardest part of any journey is the beginning, and we have taken that step through our total commitment to recovery.

Our spiritual awakening is a gift that instills in us a new perspective. It is usually accompanied by a positive and significant change in our value systems. Our pursuit of worldly goals has been subdued and redirected; we now look for fulfillment from things of real and lasting values. For most of us, the awakening is subtle and best seen in hindsight. It is seldom a single and distinct beginning and ending. Jesus comes to us when and as He wants. We also realize it took all of this to get us here; that's why we were asleep for so long. As we awaken to the presence of God's love for us, our lives become filled with new purpose and meaning. In Romans 13:11, Paul tells us: "The hour has come for you to wake up from your slumber, because our salvation is nearer now than when we first believed."

Personal Reflection

"Actions speak louder than words" is an accurate description of how we should carry the Twelve Step message to others. It is more effective to witness a principle being applied than to hear lectures on theory alone. For example, sharing our own experiences of prayer and meditation has more meaning than simply lecturing and explaining why everyone should meditate and pray. We can most effectively carry the message by sharing our own experiences of a spiritual life through working the Steps. Telling our story will help others recognize their need and encourage the growth of our own humility. Carrying the message gives us an opportunity to describe the ways in which the Twelve Steps have transformed our lives and renewed our relationship with God. Through our sharing, we can explain how our lives have been transformed by our work with the Twelve Steps.

- Describe a recent situation in which you carried the Twelve Step message to another person merely by your actions and example. _____

_____

_____

_____

- How have the Twelve Steps transformed your life and renewed your relationship with God? _____

_____

_____

_____

PHILIPPIANS 4:8-9
Finally, brothers, whatever is true, whatever is noble, whatever is right, whatever is pure, whatever is lovely, whatever is admirable—if anything is excellent or praiseworthy—think about such things. Whatever you have learned or received or heard from me, or seen in me—put it into practice. And the God of peace will be with you.

- Describe a praiseworthy thing you have accomplished; indicate why you believe this can be an example of God working through you, and can help others discover the same blessings in their lives. _____

  _____

  _____

  _____

♦ ♦ ♦

Scripture contains dramatic examples of the results of personal testimony about God's interaction in human affairs. John 4:28 and John 9:17 are accounts of personal experiences with Jesus Christ and their impact on the lives of others. Those who knew the speakers were convinced of the force of Christ's presence by the changes they observed. We cannot separate Twelve Step work from our Christian walk; they are connected by our Lord's guiding hand. The action segment of the Twelfth Step is perfectly described in Romans 10:10: "For it is with your heart that you believe and are justified, and it is with your mouth that you confess and are saved."

- What connection do you see between the Twelve Steps and your Christian walk? _____

  _____

  _____

  _____

COLOSSIANS 4:5-6

Be wise in the way you act toward outsiders; make the most of every opportunity. Let your conversation be always full of grace, seasoned with salt, so that you may know how to answer everyone.

- Cite a recent situation in which you made a newcomer to recovery feel comfortable. How did the grace of God support this? _____

  _____

  _____

  _____

MARK 5:19

Jesus did not let him, but said, "Go home to your family and tell them how much the Lord has done for you, and how he has had mercy on you."

- How has the Lord and His examples helped you spread the message of the Twelve Steps?

  _____

  _____

  _____

  _____

♦ ♦ ♦

Working with newcomers in using the Spiritual 12 Steps can be very rewarding. Many of them are troubled, confused and resentful. They need guidance and help to understand that the Program, through their hard work and commitment, will produce rewards and miracles that far outweigh their present pain. We must encourage newcomers to be gentle with themselves and to work the Program one day at a time. This can be a growth experience for us. As we reflect on where we were when first introduced to the Program, we see how far we have come. When carrying the message, we must emphasize that the decision to join the Program is usually made when we have suffered enough, are discouraged, are tired of hurting and have "hit bottom."

- Cite a recent situation in which you helped a newcomer. Describe your feelings that resulted from this? _____
_____
_____
_____

2 TIMOTHY 4:2
Preach the word; be prepared in season and out of season; correct, rebuke and encourage—with great patience and careful instruction.

- What do you most comfortably tell newcomers that encourages them? _____
_____
_____
_____

EPHESIANS 5:1-2
Be imitators of God, therefore, as dearly loved children and live a life of love, just as Christ loved us and gave himself up for us as a fragrant offering and sacrifice to God.

- How does practicing these principles exemplify Christ's love at work and help you carry this message to others? _____
_____
_____
_____

♦ ♦ ♦

Our relationship with God is the key to our success in working the Steps and applying the principles in our daily affairs. We cannot allow ourselves to drift into indifference and neglect our commitment to living according to the teachings of Christ. Scripture reminds us of the mandate to live a Christ-like life, and tells us how we will know if we fail: "No one who lives in Him keeps on sinning. No one who continues to sin has either seen Him or known Him." (1 John 3:6) Life constantly reminds us that we must be prepared to face temptations and trials and, with God's help, transform them into occasions for growth and comfort to ourselves and to those around us. We must understand that we will never achieve peace and serenity independently of God's grace.

● How has God's grace helped you to use the Twelve Steps as a way to achieve peace and serenity? _____

_____

_____

_____

1 PETER 4:11

> *If anyone speaks, he should do it as one speaking the very words of God. If anyone serves, he should do it with the strength God provides, so that in all things God may be praised through Jesus Christ. To him be the glory and the power forever and ever. Amen.*

● How does your relationship with God help you to practice the principles of the Steps in all your affairs? _____

_____

_____

_____

◆ ◆ ◆

Sometimes we become discouraged and lose sight of our progress. If this happens, we compare our past to our present and ask ourselves:

- Are we less isolated and no longer afraid of people in authority?
- Have we stopped seeking approval from others and accepted ourselves as we really are?
- Are we more selective of the people with whom we develop relationships, and more able to keep our own identity while in a relationship?
- Have we developed the ability to express our feelings?
- Have we stopped trying to dominate others?
- Are we no longer behaving childishly by turning friends or spouses into protective parents and being overly dependent?
- Have we become attentive to the needs of our inner-child?

Affirmative answers indicate the extent of our progress toward a healthier and better way of living.

● Which of the above situations is still causing you difficulty? Explain. _____

_____

_____

_____

● With which of the above situations have you been most successful in changing your behavior toward healthier relating? _____

_____

_____

_____

GALATIANS 6:1

> *Brother, if someone is caught in a sin, you who are spiritual should restore him gently. But watch yourself, or you also may be tempted.*

● Cite an example in which you realized that someone was behaving inappropriately and you were able to help that person take corrective action. _____

_____

_____

_____

◆ ◆ ◆

An important achievement in working the Steps occurs when we become accustomed to "living" the Steps. We do this by habitually taking a problem or concern through the Steps, while acknowledging our need for God's support and guidance. The resulting peace and serenity provide a threshold of competence from which we can deal directly with the problem. Any action we take is then clearly guided by God's hand and our honest appraisal of the consequences. We can act confidently and without fear, affirming "The Lord is my light and my salvation—whom shall I fear? The Lord is the stronghold of my life—of whom shall I be afraid?" (Psalm 6:29)

● Cite an example of your "living" the Steps. _____

_____

_____

_____

● List a recent concern you have had and describe your experience of working it out by applying the Twelve Steps. _____

_____

_____

_____

ECCLESIASTES 4:9-11

> *Two are better than one, because they have a good return for their work: If one falls down, his friend can help him up. But pity the man who falls and has no one to help him up! Also, if two lie down together, they will keep warm. But how can one keep warm alone?*

● Describe a situation in which you and another person shared the Twelve-Step message with someone who needed help. What resulted from your efforts? _____

_____

_____

_____

◆ ◆ ◆

At this point, we begin to identify the many areas of our lives that are being affected by working the Twelve Steps. Our success with handling new problems is linked to our willingness to thoughtfully take action, while remembering to let go and turn it over to God. Our faith grows as we learn to relinquish control and allow God to be the director of our lives. The process is gradual, regenerative and never-ending. We slowly become more God-centered as we learn the true meaning of love, peace and serenity. Paul captured the dynamic of this Twelve Step process when he said: "Brothers, I do not consider myself yet to have taken hold of it. But one thing I do: Forgetting what is behind and straining toward what is ahead, I press on toward the goal to win the prize for which God has called me heavenward in Christ Jesus." (Philippians 3:13-14)

- Describe a current situation in your life in which you see God as directing the course of activity. _____

_____

_____

_____

LUKE 8:16-18

"No one lights a lamp and hides it in a jar or puts it under a bed. Instead, he puts it on a stand, so that those who come in can see the light. For there is nothing hidden that will not be disclosed, and nothing concealed that will not be known or brought out into the open. Therefore consider carefully how you listen. Whoever has will be given more; whoever does not have, even what he thinks he has will be taken from him."

- Explain how you experience God's Holy Spirit guiding your new behavior; in what way do you believe it is positively influencing the lives of others? _____

_____

_____

_____

Each new day is a gift from God that we can accept and acknowledge joyfully as an answer to our prayer for serenity.

PRAYER FOR SERENITY

God, grant me the serenity
to accept the things I cannot change,
the courage to change the things I can,
and the wisdom to know the difference.
Living one day at a time,
enjoying one moment at a time;
accepting hardship as a pathway to peace;
taking, as Jesus did,
this sinful world as it is,
not as I would have it;
trusting that You will make all things right
if I surrender to your will;
so that I may be reasonably happy in this life
and supremely happy with You forever in the next.
AMEN

Reinhold Niebuhr

TWELVE STEP EXERCISE

- Identify a situation or condition in your life that is currently a source of resentment, fear, sadness or anger. It may involve relationships (family, work or sexual), work environment, health or self-esteem. Write a concise statement describing the situation and indicating your concern. _____

_____

_____

Use the following exercise to apply the principles of the Twelve Steps to the above.

- **Step One:** In what ways are you powerless, and how is this situation showing you the unmanageability of your life? _____

_____

_____

_____

- **Step Two:** How do you see your Higher Power as helping to restore you to sanity? _____

_____

_____

_____

- **Step Three:** How does being willing to turn your life over to the care of God assist you in dealing with this? _____

_____

_____

_____

- **Step Four:** What character defects have surfaced (e.g., fear of abandonment or authority figures, control, approval seeking, obsessive/compulsive behavior, rescuing, excessive responsibility, unexpressed feelings)? _____

_____

_____

_____

- **Step Five:** Admit your wrongs, at least to God and yourself. _____

_____

_____

_____

- **Step Six:** Are you entirely ready to have God remove the character defects that have surfaced? If not, explain: _____
_____
_____
_____

- **Step Seven:** Can you humbly submit to God and ask Him to remove your shortcomings? If not, why do you resist? _____
_____
_____
_____

- **Step Eight:** Make a list of the persons being harmed. _____
_____
_____
_____

- **Step Nine:** What amends are necessary, and how will you make amends? _____
_____
_____
_____

- **Step Ten:** Review the above Steps to be sure that nothing has been overlooked. _____
_____
_____
_____

- **Step Eleven:** Take a moment for prayer or meditation, asking God for knowledge of His will for you. What is your understanding of God's will in this situation? _____
_____
_____
_____

- **Step Twelve:** How can your understanding and spiritual awakening assist you in dealing with your problem? _____
_____
_____
_____

APPENDIX ONE

Methods of Study

There are two methods for using this workbook effectively: self-study and group study. Use this appendix as a guide to assist you in successfully completing the workbook. The information contained in the self-study section also applies to group study.

Self-Study

Read the entire Step narrative for each Step before reading the questions. Then turn to the personal reflection section and answer the questions. This will give you a better perspective of the overall scope of the material being presented. Don't be discouraged if Steps One, Two and Three seem overwhelming to you—this is a common reaction for persons who are new to the Steps. Completion of these three Steps forms the foundation for working the Program.

As you proceed through the Steps, it is important to pace yourself. Work on each Step until it is completed, and allow sufficient time to complete each process. This may take a day, a week or longer. Be patient with yourself; allow ample time to digest the content of each Step and reflect on its meaning. Impatience can seriously impair your effectiveness.

Depending upon the degree of serenity you achieve and maintain, you may decide to go through the Step Study more than once. The Program is a lifelong process to be used in part or in whole on a daily basis. This workbook should not be your only involvement; it is just one part of working the Twelve Steps.

Wherever possible, share your insights with someone you trust. Communicating your discoveries to another human being can work miracles. In many Anonymous programs, this person is referred to as a sponsor. Sponsors are familiar with the Steps, and their insights and experiences can be invaluable; but be aware that your listener is not there to give advice or to heal you. The healing results from your relationship with the Lord.

If this workbook is your first exposure to the Twelve Steps and you are not presently participating in an Anonymous Twelve Step Program, it is important that you find a meeting to attend. The **Self-Help Resources** listed in this Appendix will help you identify the program for you. Other resources are available. Check your library or the telephone directory under "social service organizations" or "crisis intervention."

Group Study

Once you have identified a Twelve Step Group with which you are comfortable, you can begin a committed Step Study Writing Workshop. The following information will assist you in forming the workshop. Appendix Two includes **Sample Meeting Guidelines for Secretary** to assist the secretary in conducting the meeting. The focus of this information is on using the workbook. Additional reading material that can be included in the workshop is available from other sources. See Appendix Seven for a list of suggested reading.

Starting a Step Study is not difficult. It involves making an announcement at one or more Anonymous meetings (Appendix One includes a **Sample Meeting Announcement).** Some people will attend only once or twice to examine the meeting and decide not to return. It is suggested that the meeting be closed to newcomers in the third week. The workshop is designed to last twenty-eight weeks, in accordance with the Appendix Three weekly writing exercises.

Even though you start the workshop and may function as secretary, be sure to have a different leader each week. It is recommended that leadership rotate by "family group" rather than by individuals. This gives each "family group" an opportunity to provide leadership periodically. The meeting formats included in Appendix Two have proven to be effective, but they are intended as suggestions only. Keep the format simple so workshop participants can focus on working the Steps.

Previous workshops have revealed that trust develops most quickly in small "family groups" with a maximum of seven individuals. For example, if twenty-four people participate, it is recommended that the workshop be divided into four "family groups" with six members each. The "family groups" will congregate to complete the evening's writing exercise and to share within their group for a specified period. The final portion of the meeting is devoted to sharing in one all-inclusive group. There is no ideal arrangement, other than keeping the "family groups" small.

When people gather to work on material as challenging as the Steps, agreement regarding the commitment to work is important. The **Participation Agreement** in Appendix Two, which is read and signed by each individual, supports this commitment.

During the workshop, various issues will surface. Perhaps dissension within the small groups will cause incompatibility. In many previous workshops, these issues were resolved without making changes within the group. The struggles within each family group were found to be re-enactments of original family situations. Leaving the groups intact for the duration of the workshop allows participants to resolve their conflicts, fosters growth and strengthens the bonds within the family group.

As participants surrender to guidance from God, many problems will be handled in a more constructive manner. As Adult Children, we are inclined to be caretakers, enablers and people-pleasers, indicated by our inability to confront inappropriate, hurtful or self-destructive behavior. Instead, we tend to be overly nice to each other. In keeping with the desire for a safe environment, excessive confrontation is usually not needed for the family group members to alter old patterns of behavior. However, straightforward feedback is critically important, with communication being limited to each one's personal experience in a given situation.

Due to our early exposure to negative behavior (e.g., resentment, greed, sexual abuse, dishonesty, gluttony, envy, laziness) and negative feelings (e.g., self-pity, sadness, insecurity, worry, fear of rejection, fear of abandonment), these patterns may seem normal to us. As we progress through the Steps, this habit of seeing negative behavior as normal will change. We will experience growth in all areas by increasing our feelings of self-worth and self-esteem. Therefore, positive feelings and thoughts need to be appreciated and encouraged. Take time during the workshop to ask for people's feelings about personal and group progress in the workshop. This enables the facilitator to encourage open, honest communication within the entire group, and to air elements of discouragement or distress before they hinder the group's progress.

There is no "right" way to work the material. Each person has something to contribute in whatever way feels most comfortable. Results will be varied, but each participant will experience growth and change. If this is your first experience in a committed Step Study Writing Workshop, you are encouraged to be in touch with individuals who are familiar with this material. Please feel free to contact us at (619) 275-1350 or write the publisher if you have any questions regarding the Step Study.

SELF-HELP RESOURCES

SECULAR GROUPS

Adult Children of Alcoholics
Central Service Board
P.O. Box 3216
Torrance, California 90505
(213) 534-1815

Al-Anon/Alateen
Family Group Headquarters, Inc.
Madison Square Station
New York, New York 10010
(212) 683-1771

Alcoholics Anonymous
World Services, Inc.
468 Park Avenue South
New York, New York 10016
(212) 686-1100

Co-Dependents Anonymous
P.O. Box 33577
Phoenix, Arizona 85067-3577
(602) 944-0141

Debtors Anonymous
P.O. Box 20322
New York, New York 10025-9992

Emotions Anonymous
P.O. Box 4245
St. Paul, Minnesota 55104

Gamblers Anonymous
P.O. Box 17173
Los Angeles, California 90017

Narcotics Anonymous
World Service Office
16155 Wyandotte Street
Van Nuys, California 91406
(818) 780-3951

National Association for
Children of Alcoholics
31706 Coast Highway, Suite 201
South Laguna, California 92677
(714) 499-3889

Overeaters Anonymous
World Service Office
2190 190th Street
Torrance, California 90504
(213) 320-7941

Sexaholics Anonymous
P.O. Box 300
Simi Valley, California 93062

CHRISTIAN GROUPS

Alcoholics for Christ
1316 N. Campbell Rd.
Royal Oak, MI 48067
(800) 441-7877

Alcoholics Victorious
National Headquarters
9370 S.W. Greenburg Rd., Suite 411
Tigard, Oregon 97323
(503) 245-9629

Changing Lives Ministries
8196 Grapewin
P.O. Box 2325
Corona, CA 91718
(714) 734-4300

Christian Alcoholics
Rehabilitation Association
FOA Road
Pocahontas, Mississippi 39072

Liontamers
2801 North Brea Blvd.
Fullerton, California 92635-2799
(714) 529-5544

New Hope
FEFC Fullerton
2801 North Brea Boulevard
Fullerton, California 92635
(714) 529-5544

New Life Treatment Center
P.O. Box 38
Woodstock, Minnesota 56186

Overcomers Outreach, Inc.
2290 West Whittier Blvd.
La Habra, California 90631
(213) 697-3994

Substance Abusers Victorious
One Cascade Plaza
Akron, Ohio 44308

SAMPLE MEETING ANNOUNCEMENT

STEP STUDY WRITING WORKSHOP
BASED ON
THE TWELVE STEPS—A SPIRITUAL JOURNEY

The First Church of Santa Barbara is sponsoring a Step Study Writing Workshop for individuals who grew up in emotionally repressive and dysfunctional families. This workshop uses the Twelve Steps in a Christian context.

Beginning Date: June 8, 1988   **Day:** Wednesday   **Time:** 7:00 to 9:00 P.M.

Location of Meeting: 305 East "A" Street, Santa Barbara

Contact Person: Susanne   **Phone:** (805) 555-1212

The Twelve Steps—A Spiritual Journey is a working guide based on Bible truths, and emphasizes self-understanding and the unchanging love of God for all humanity. This book:

- offers a tool to restore the fruits of the Spirit in your life; joy, peace, gentleness, goodness and faith.

- provides a workable formula for confronting the past and surrendering one's life to God.

- reaffirms the dominion of God over all of life.

- emphasizes the relationship between The Twelve Steps and the practice of Christianity.

◆ ◆ ◆

STEP STUDY WRITING WORKSHOP OVERVIEW

Following is an outline of what to expect from participating in a Step Study Writing Workshop using the book *The Twelve Steps—A Spiritual Journey* ($14.95).

- During the first three weeks, the meeting remains open so that anyone interested in experiencing the meeting format is welcomed to do so.

- After the third week (the date being _____), small family groups are formed. These groups are an important part of the Step Study process and encourage the development of trusting, supportive relationships during the weeks that follow.

- Beginning with the fourth week, the meeting is facilitated by each family group on a rotating basis. The meeting format is in Appendix Two of the workbook.

- Two weeks are devoted to completing most of the Steps.

- Read the workbook material and complete as much of the writing as possible in a timely manner.

- The writing exercise for each Step (Appendix Three), is the focus of the weekly meeting. Time is spent at the beginning of the meeting to complete the exercise, which then becomes the basis for family sharing.

- Remember that you are doing this work for your own personal growth. Set your own pace and accept your progress without having unrealistic expectations of yourself.

- This program is worked most successfully one day at a time.

SAMPLE MEETING SCHEDULE

STEP STUDY WRITING WORKSHOP
THE TWELVE STEPS—A SPIRITUAL JOURNEY
PROGRAM SCHEDULE

WEEK	DATE	IN-CLASS EXERCISES	AT-HOME WORK
Intro Week 1	6/8	Workshop Overview	Characteristics
Intro Week 2	6/15	Overview & Writing	Step One
Intro Week 3	6/29	Step 1 Week 1	Step One
4 (Closed)	7/6	Step 1 Week 2	Step Two
5	7/13	Step 2 Week 1	Step Two
6	7/20	Step 2 Week 2	Step Three
7	7/27	Step 3 Week 1	Step Three
8	8/3	Step 3 Week 2	Step Four
9	8/10	Step 4 Week 1	Step Four
10	8/17	Step 4 Week 2	Step Four
11	8/24	Step 4 Week 3	Step Five
12	8/31	Step 5 Week 1	Step Five
13	9/7	Step 5 Week 2	Get Current
14	9/14	*Special Program*	Step Six
15	9/21	Step 6 Week 1	Step Seven
16	9/28	Step 7 Week 1	Step Eight
17	10/5	Step 8 Week 1	Step Eight
18	10/12	Step 8 Week 2	Step Nine
19	10/19	Step 9 Week 1	Step Nine
20	10/26	Step 9 Week 2	Step Ten
21	11/2	Step 10 Week 1	Step Ten
22	11/9	Step 10 Week 2	Step Eleven
23	11/16	Step 11 Week 1	Step Eleven
24	11/23	Step 11 Week 2	Get Current
25	11/30	*Special Program*	Step Twelve
26	12/7	Step 12 Week 1	Step Twelve
27	12/14	Step 12 Week 2	
28	12/21	*Closing Meeting*	

The process of working the Steps can be compared to the transformation of a caterpillar into a butterfly. The caterpillar is not clear that it is going to be a butterfly. Every part of its death and rebirth in the cocoon must be experienced.

The story is told of a man who noticed a cocoon on a bush in his yard. As he started to remove it from the bush and throw it away, he noticed the end was opening and a butterfly was struggling to escape. In an effort to help the emerging butterfly, he took it inside and carefully cut the cocoon away with a razor blade. The butterfly feebly crawled away from the open cocoon and, within a few hours, died. It needed the strength it would have gained from the struggle to free itself in order to survive in the outside world.

Working the Steps is something that only we can do. Any attempt to have another person do our work or find answers for us inhibits our own recovery and limits our ability to become strong.

APPENDIX TWO

PRAYER FOR SERENITY

God, grant me the serenity
to accept the things I cannot change,
the courage to change the things I can,
and the wisdom to know the difference.
Living one day at a time,
enjoying one moment at a time;
accepting hardship as a pathway to peace;
taking, as Jesus did,
this sinful world as it is,
not as I would have it;
trusting that You will make all things right
if I surrender to your will;
so that I may be reasonably happy in this life
and supremely happy with You forever in the next.
AMEN

Reinhold Niebuhr

MILESTONES IN RECOVERY

Through God's help and our work in the Twelve Step Program, we can look forward to achieving the following milestones in recovery.

- We feel comfortable with people, including authority figures.
- We have a strong identity and generally approve of ourselves.
- We accept and use personal criticism in a positive way.
- As we face our own life situation, we find we are attracted by strengths and understand the weaknesses in our relationships with other people.
- We are recovering through loving and focusing on ourselves; we accept responsibility for our own thoughts and actions.
- We feel comfortable standing up for ourselves when it is appropriate.
- We are enjoying peace and serenity, trusting that God is guiding our recovery.
- We love people who love and take care of themselves.
- We are free to feel and express our feelings even when they cause us pain.
- We have a healthy sense of self-esteem.
- We are developing new skills that allow us to initiate and complete ideas and projects.
- We take prudent action by first considering alternative behaviors and possible consequences.
- We rely more and more on God as our Higher Power.

THE TWELVE STEPS

STEP ONE

We admitted we were powerless over our separation from God—that our lives had become unmanageable.

STEP TWO

Came to believe that a power greater than ourselves could restore us to sanity.

STEP THREE

Made a decision to turn our will and our lives over to the care of God as we understood Him.

STEP FOUR

Made a searching and fearless moral inventory of ourselves.

STEP FIVE

Admitted to God, to ourselves, and to another human being the exact nature of our wrongs.

STEP SIX

Were entirely ready to have God remove all these defects of character.

STEP SEVEN

Humbly asked Him to remove our shortcomings.

STEP EIGHT

Made a list of all persons we had harmed and became willing to make amends to them all.

STEP NINE

Made direct amends to such people wherever possible, except when to do so would injure them or others.

STEP TEN

Continued to take personal inventory and, when we were wrong, promptly admitted it.

STEP ELEVEN

Sought through prayer and meditation to improve our conscious contact with God as we understood Him, praying only for knowledge of His will for us and the power to carry that out.

STEP TWELVE

Having had a spiritual awakening as the result of these steps, we tried to carry this message to others, and to practice these principles in all our affairs.

SCRIPTURE FOR THE TWELVE STEPS

STEP ONE

I know nothing good lives in me, that is, in my sinful nature. For I have the desire to do what is good, but I cannot carry it out. (Romans 7:18)

STEP TWO

For it is God who works in you to will and to act according to his good purpose. (Philippians 2:13)

STEP THREE

Therefore, I urge you, brothers, in view of God's mercy, to offer your bodies as living sacrifices, holy and pleasing to God—which is your spiritual worship. (Romans 12:1)

STEP FOUR

Let us examine our ways and test them, and let us return to the Lord. (Lamentations 3:40)

STEP FIVE

Therefore confess your sins to each other and pray for each other so that you may be healed. (James 5:16a)

STEP SIX

Humble yourselves before the Lord, and he will lift you up. (James 4:10)

STEP SEVEN

If we confess our sins, he is faithful and just and will forgive us our sins and purify us from all unrighteousness. (1 John 1:9)

STEP EIGHT

Do to others as you would have them do to you. (Luke 6:31)

STEP NINE

Therefore, if you are offering your gift at the altar and there remember that your brother has something against you, leave your gift there in front of the altar. First go and be reconciled to your brother; then come and offer your gift. (Matthew 5:23-24)

STEP TEN

So, if you think you are standing firm, be careful that you don't fall. (1 Corinthians 10:12)

STEP ELEVEN

Let the word of Christ dwell in you richly. (Colossians 3:16a)

STEP TWELVE

Brothers, if someone is caught in a sin, you who are spiritual should restore him gently. But watch yourself, or you also may be tempted. (Galatians 6:1)

SAMPLE STEP STUDY WRITING WORKSHOP PARTICIPATION AGREEMENT

I, _____ , agree to participate with my family in working the Twelve Steps and also agree to:

- Give my maximum effort by actively participating in weekly meetings and maintaining contact with my Step Study family between meetings.

- Be as confident as possible, relying on God for help and healing.

- Support my family group by giving each person my undivided attention.

- Be as honest as possible in all things.

- Openly share my uncomfortable feelings when someone makes offensive comments or uses inappropriate language.

- Humbly submit to the process and do my best to suspend negative judgment.

- Schedule time between weekly meetings to complete the written work on the Step and to study the Step as thoroughly as possible.

- Accept the discomfort and unsettling behavior changes which may accompany working the Twelve Steps.

- Keep my commitment to myself and to my family group by regularly attending the weekly meetings.

- Share my experience, strength, and hope during the meeting.

- Refrain from trying to "explain" situations when sharing, and do my best to clearly identify and share my feelings (e.g., joy, sadness, depression, anger, love, hate, guilt, loneliness, inadequacy).

- Incorporate the "Five Practices of Recovery" into my daily life by:
  - Attending meetings.
  - Working the Steps.
  - Praying and meditating daily.
  - Using the telephone to maintain contact with members of my family group.
  - Beginning and ending each day with the first three Steps.

COMMON BEHAVIOR CHARACTERISTICS OF ADULT CHILDREN

- We have feelings of low self-esteem that cause us to judge ourselves and others without mercy. We try to cover up or compensate by being perfectionistic, caretaking, controlling, contemptuous and gossipy.

- We tend to isolate ourselves and to feel uneasy around other people, especially authority figures.

- We are approval seekers and will do anything to make people like us. We are extremely loyal, even when evidence indicates loyalty is undeserved.

- We are intimidated by angry people and personal criticism. This causes us to feel anxious and overly sensitive.

- We habitually choose to have relationships with emotionally unavailable people with addictive personalities. We are usually less attracted to healthy, caring people.

- We live life as victims and are attracted to other victims in our love and friendship relationships. We confuse love with pity and tend to "love" people we can pity and rescue.

- We are either super-responsible or super-irresponsible. We try to solve others' problems or expect others to be responsible for us. This enables us to avoid looking closely at our own behavior.

- We feel guilty when we stand up for ourselves or act assertively. We give in to others instead of taking care of ourselves.

- We deny, minimize or repress our feelings from our traumatic childhoods. We lose the ability to express our feelings and are unaware of the impact this has on our lives.

- We are dependent personalities who are terrified of rejection or abandonment. We tend to stay in jobs or relationships that are harmful to us. Our fears can either stop us from ending hurtful relationships or prevent us from entering into healthy, rewarding ones.

- Denial, isolation, control and misplaced guilt are symptoms of family dysfunction. As a result of these behaviors, we feel hopeless and helpless.

- We have difficulty with intimate relationships. We feel insecure and lack trust in others. We don't have clearly defined boundaries and become enmeshed with our partner's needs and emotions.

- We have difficulty following projects through from beginning to end.

- We have a strong need to be in control. We over-react to change over which we have no control.

- We tend to be impulsive. We take action before considering alternative behaviors or possible consequences.

SAMPLE STEP STUDY WRITING WORKSHOP FORMAT
INTRODUCTORY MEETING—WEEK 1

For those who do not have workbooks, have copies of:

- *Step Study Writing Workshop Overview (page 151).*
- *Step One narrative (pages 5-6).*
- *The Twelve Steps and Your Spiritual Pilgrimage (page ix).*
- *Common Behavior Characteristics of Adult Children (pages 1-4)*
- *Week #2 writing exercise (page 171)*

[Reward promptness by starting the meeting on time.]

7:00 [Allow approximately 25 minutes for the following.]

[Pass out *Common Behavior Characteristics of Adult Children, Milestones in Recovery, The Twelve Steps* and *Scripture for The Twelve Steps.*]

"Good evening! Welcome to the _____ Step Study Writing Workshop. My name is _____ , and I am an Adult Child. During my childhood, I was influenced by a dysfunctional family environment in which addictive, compulsive or obsessive behavior of an adult seriously damaged me. As a result, my self-esteem was negatively affected. I recognize that dysfunctional behavior is generational, and it is my intention to stop it in my lifetime."

"It is possible to have the characteristics of an Adult Child without having biological parents who are, themselves, chemically dependent, outwardly abusive or violent. The characteristics could have been passed down by grandparents or significant others in our lives."

"As we begin our time together, please join me for a moment of silence, followed by the Serenity Prayer."

"I have asked _____ to read ***Common Behavior Characteristics of Adult Children.***"

"I have asked _____ to read ***The Twelve Steps.***"

"I have asked _____ to read ***Scripture for The Twelve Steps*** after each Step."

"I have asked _____ to read ***Milestones in Recovery.***"

"Our tradition is to be self-supporting through our own monetary contributions. We ask for your contribution at this time to avoid interrupting the meeting."

[After the collection]:

"Please introduce yourself by giving your first name only. This respects the anonymity of those who are present. It is not a requirement that you disclose your identity."

[After the introduction]:

"I welcome each of you. A Step Study Writing Workshop is not easy. You will find that the writing we do on each of the Twelve Steps is a powerful healing tool. Working the Steps can be extremely difficult in the beginning stages of your recovery. We suggest you attend other meetings, open step study meetings and read additional materials relating to Adult Children. This will broaden your understanding and enhance your ability to participate in the Twelve

Step process. One of the first lessons in recovery is to know your own limitations and participate only in those activities that support your recovery."

"During the first three weeks, you will have an opportunity to experience the process used in this workshop. You will be asked to make a decision about your personal commitment by the third meeting. The full program requires twenty-eight weeks of work, study, reflection and growth."

"You will find new relationships opening up to you as you spend time with the group and share experiences, strengths and hopes. The quality of these relationships may be unlike any other you have experienced."

"The principal purpose of this workshop is to facilitate healing and recovery. You will be asked to do some unfamiliar things, such as trusting others, practicing healthy dependence and interdependence, listening carefully and sharing your feelings. You will have the opportunity to experience what life within a healthy family can be."

7:25 [Allow approximately 30 minutes for the following.]

[Have copies of the *Step Study Writing Workshop Overview* available to distribute.]

[Read the *Step Study Writing Workshop Overview* aloud.]

"As the facilitator of this meeting, I will lead only the first three meetings. By the fourth meeting, family groups will have been formed, and each group will be responsible for leading the meeting on a rotating basis."

"This is an introductory meeting intended to provide an overview of the Step Study Writing Workshop using *The Twelve Steps—A Spiritual Journey.*"

[Have copies of *Step One* narrative (first two pages) and *The Twelve Steps and Your Spiritual Pilgrimage* available to distribute.]

"For those of you who have not purchased a copy of the workbook, I have a sample from *Step One* narrative and a copy of *The Twelve Steps and Your Spiritual Pilgrimage.* For those who have the workbook, please turn to Step One and we will review the format of the writing to be done between the weekly meetings."

[Select material from *Step One* narrative to be read out loud.]

"Before attempting to write responses to the questions relating to each Step, read the entire step narrative for an overview of the material. Reading the Step narrative and responding to the questions prior to the meeting will significantly improve the value you will receive from participating in the Step Study."

[Select material from *The Twelve Steps and Your Spiritual Pilgrimage* to be read aloud.]

"The Steps are a process that prepares you to allow God to remove behavior which is harmful to yourself and to others. Your willingness to commit to this workshop will help you make changes in your behavior. Do not be too concerned with the writing. Do the best you can and work at your own pace. There are no right or wrong answers, and no right or wrong ways to complete the exercises."

"As the facilitator of the meeting, my purpose is to be your trusted servant. I will work the Steps with you. Understand that I am here, as I believe you are, to share my experience, strength and hope."

"The principal commitment required to successfully complete this work is a willingness to engage in the process one day at a time, one meeting at a time. It is also vital to trust God to take care of the outcome."

7:55 [Allow approximately 20 minutes for the following.]

"We will spend the next 20 minutes discussing what we just reviewed and *The Twelve Steps and Your Spiritual Pilgrimage.*"

8:15 [Allow approximately 35 minutes for the following.]

[End of first discussion period]:

[Have copies of the *Week #2* writing exercise available to distribute.]

"For those who do not have the workbook, I am going to distribute a sample of the *Week #2* writing exercise."

"Approximately ten minutes is allocated to the writing exercise during each Step Study meeting, followed by approximately forty-five minutes of "family group" sharing. The sharing is either about the evening's writing exercise or the writing in the workbook."

"Following the family group sharing, the meeting is open for discussion including all family groups. Approximately thirty minutes is spent on general sharing."

"The meeting lasts from 7:00 to 9:00, approximately two hours."

"At this time the meeting is open for further discussion on miscellaneous questions relative to the workshop."

8:50 [Allow approximately 10 minutes to conclude the meeting.]

[End of group sharing]:

"The material that will be used from the workbook each week will guide you through the writing processes dealing with each Step. It is not intended to provide all the possible information on each Step or Bible citation."

[Have a copy of *Common Behavior Characteristics of Adult Children* available to distribute.]

"For the meeting next week, please read and respond to the questions from *Common Behavior Characteristics of Adult Children.* Our writing and discussion will focus on this material."

[Ask for any announcements.]

"Reminder! What you hear at this meeting is confidential; leave it at this meeting! It is not for public disclosure or gossip. Please respect the privacy of those who shared with us tonight."

"Will everyone please clean up after themselves and help rearrange the room?"

"Will all who care to, please join me in the closing prayer?"

9:00 [Adjourn.]

SAMPLE STEP STUDY WRITING WORKSHOP FORMAT
INTRODUCTORY MEETING—WEEK 2

For those who do not have workbooks, have copies of:

- *Step Study Writing Workshop overview (page 151).*
- *The Twelve Steps and Your Spiritual Pilgrimage (page ix).*
- *Common Behavior Characteristics of Adult Children (pages 1-4)*
- *Week #2 writing exercise (page 171).*

[Reward promptness by starting the meeting on time.]

7:00 [Allow approximately 25 minutes for the following.]

[Pass out *Common Behavior Characteristics of Adult Children, Milestones in Recovery, The Twelve Steps* and *Scripture For The Twelve Steps.*]

"Good evening! Welcome to the _____ Step Study Writing Workshop. My name is _____ , and I am an Adult Child. During my childhood, I was influenced by a dysfunctional family environment in which addictive, compulsive or obsessive behavior of an adult seriously damaged me. As a result, my self-esteem was negatively affected. I recognize that dysfunctional behavior is generational, and it is my intention to stop it in my lifetime."

"It is possible to have the characteristics of an Adult Child without having biological parents who are, themselves, chemically dependent, outwardly abusive or violent. The characteristics could have been passed down by grandparents or significant others in our lives."

"As we begin our time together, please join me for a moment of silence, followed by the Serenity Prayer."

"I have asked _____ to read *Common Behavior Characteristics of Adult Children.*"

"I have asked _____ to read *The Twelve Steps.*"

"I have asked _____ to read *Scripture for The Twelve Steps* after each Step."

"I have asked _____ to read *Milestones in Recovery.*"

"Our tradition is to be self-supporting through our own monetary contributions. We ask for your contribution at this time to avoid interrupting the meeting."

[After the collection]:

"Please introduce yourself by giving your first name only. This respects the anonymity of those who are present. You are not required to disclose your identity."

[After the introduction]:

"I welcome each of you. A Step Study Workshop is not easy. You will find that the writing we do on each of the Twelve Steps is a powerful healing tool. Working the Steps can be extremely difficult in the beginning stages of your recovery. We suggest you attend other meetings, open step study meetings and read additional materials relating to Adult Children. This will broaden your understanding and enhance your ability to participate in the Twelve Step process. One of the first lessons in recovery is to know your own limitations and participate only in those activities that support your recovery."

"During this meeting and the one next week, you will have an opportunity to experience the process used in this workshop. You will be asked to make a decision about your personal commitment by the third meeting. The full program requires twenty-eight weeks of work, study, reflection and growth."

"You will find new relationships opening up to you as you spend time with the group and share experiences, strengths and hopes. The quality of these relationships may be unlike any other you have experienced."

"The principal purpose of this workshop is to facilitate healing and recovery. You will be asked to do some unfamiliar things, such as trusting others, practicing healthy dependence and interdependence, listening carefullly and sharing your feelings. You will have the opportunity to experience what life within a healthy family can be."

"If you decide to join this writing workshop, you will be asked to make the following commitments.

- Make a sincere effort to do the work, realizing that some of the material will cause personal discomfort.
  - Attend regularly (bring the body; the mind will follow).
  - Participate in the meeting and share to the best of your ability.
  - Take responsibility for doing what you need to do.
- Allow for change, exercising courage and patience. You don't have to do it all alone or all at once. Remember:
  - Choosing health will frequently be painful, will sometimes bring condemnation from others and will appear abnormal.
- Participate in healthy family-type interaction.
  - Tell the truth and keep your word.
  - Be willing to accept support and to give it to others.
  - In this life, we can never be more or less than fallible human beings.
  - Identify and accept your limits and the limits of others—physically, mentally, and emotionally.
- Accept the fact that this is a spiritual program, born of the realization that trust and reliance on our Higher Power is life-changing and life-affirming.
  - Recognize that healing is done by the Power of God's Holy Spirit.
  - Accept that God is committed to using imperfection to achieve His purposes for His children.
  - Surrender to the fact that we are all equal recipients of the Love of God we receive through Jesus Christ.
- Engage in "recovery-type" sharing as distinguished from "dumping."
  - Express "recovery-type" sharing by communicating how your program is working to heal old patterns of addictive, compulsive or obsessive behavior.
  - Avoid "dumping", which is stating your problems and looking at yourself as a victim, rather than as someone working a program of recovery.

7:25 [Allow approximately 10 minutes for the following.]

[Have copies of the Step Study Writing Workshop overview available to distribute.]

[Read the Step Study Writing Workshop overview and indicate in which week the meeting will be closed.]

7:35 [Allow approximately 15 minutes for the following.]

[Ask that small groups of four to six be formed, depending on the total group size.]

[Have a copy of *Common Behavior Characteristics of Adult Children* and *Week #2* writing exercise available for those who do not have the workbook.]

"Before we start the writing exercise, please read along with me *Common Behavior Characteristics of Adult Children.*"

[Prior to start of writing exercise]:

(If available, soft music is useful during the writing segment.)

"Ten minutes are allowed to complete the individual writing process. I will give a two-minute warning to allow you to complete your writing."

7:50 [Allow approximately 25 minutes for the following.]

[End of writing time]:

"Sharing your writing work within each group will last twenty-five minutes. Focus on your writing and allow everyone to share, answering one question at a time. Until everyone has shared, please don't crosstalk. "Crosstalk" is when two people enter into a dialogue that excludes other group members. Please limit your comments or observations to your own personal experience. I'll give a three-minute warning to allow you to complete the sharing."

"Try not to 'intellectualize' when sharing. To the best of your ability, share the feelings you experienced while writing (e.g., joy, sadness, anger, love, guilt, hurt, loneliness)."

8:15 [Allow approximately 35 minutes for the following.]

[End of small group sharing]:

"Please rearrange your chairs into one large circle. The meeting is now open for sharing tonight's experiences."

8:50 [Allow 10 minutes to conclude the meeting.]

[End of large group sharing]:

"The material that will be used from the workbook each week will guide you through the writing processes dealing with each Step. It is not intended to provide all the possible information on each Step or Bible citation."

"Our discussion for next week will be based upon material from Step One. I recommend purchasing a copy of *The Twelve Steps—A Spiritual Journey* if you plan to continue this workshop. Please read Step One."

[Ask for any announcements.]

"Newcomers are invited to remain after the meeting to discuss any questions they may have about the Step Study."

"Reminder! What you hear at this meeting is confidential; please leave it at this meeting! It is not for public disclosure or gossip. Please respect the privacy of the persons who have shared here tonight."

"Will everyone please clean up after themselves and help rearrange the room?"

"Will all who care to, please join me in the closing prayer?"

9:00 [Adjourn.]

SAMPLE STEP STUDY WRITING WORKSHOP FORMAT
INTRODUCTORY MEETING—WEEK 3

For those who do not have workbooks, have copies of:

- *Step Study Writing Workshop overview (page 151).*
- *Step One narrative (pages 5-6).*
- *Week #3 writing exercise (page 173).*
- *Participation agreement (page 156).*

[Have 3x5 cards available to be completed by participants.]

[Reward promptness by starting the meeting on time.]

7:00 [Allow approximately 25 minutes for the following.]

[Pass out *Common Behavior Characteristics of Adult Children, Milestones in Recovery, The Twelve Steps* and *Scripture for The Twelve Steps.]*

"Good evening! Welcome to the _____ Step Study Writing Workshop. My name is _____ , and I am an Adult Child. During my childhood, I was influenced by a dysfunctional family environment in which addictive, compulsive or obsessive behavior of an adult seriously damaged me. As a result, my own adult behavior became dysfunctional. I recognize that dysfunctional behavior is generational, and it is my intention to stop it in my lifetime."

"It is possible to have the characteristics of an Adult Child without having biological parents who are, themselves, chemically dependent, outwardly abusive or violent. The characteristics could have been passed down by grandparents or significant others in our lives."

"As we begin our time together, please join me for a moment of silence, followed by the Serenity Prayer."

"I have asked _____ to read *Common Behavior Characteristics of Adult Children.*"

"I have asked _____ to read *The Twelve Steps.*"

"I have asked _____ to read *Scripture for The Twelve Steps* after each step."

"I have asked _____ to read *Milestones in Recovery.*"

"Our tradition is to be self-supporting through our own monetary contributions. We ask for your contribution at this time to avoid interrupting the meeting."

[After the collection]:

"Please introduce yourself by giving your first name only. This respects the anonymity of those who are present. You are not required to disclose your identity."

[After introductions]:

"I welcome each of you. A Step Study Workshop is not easy. You will find that the writing we will do on each of the Twelve Steps is a powerful healing tool. Working the Steps can be extremely difficult at the beginning stages of your recovery. We suggest you attend other meetings, open step study meetings and read additional materials relating to Adult Children. This will broaden your understanding and enhance your ability to participate in the Twelve Step process. One of the first lessons in recovery is to know your own limitations and participate only in those activities that support your recovery."

"This is the last open meeting where you will have an opportunity to experience the process used in this workshop. You will be asked to make a decision about your personal commitment at this meeting. The full program requires twenty-eight weeks of work, study, reflection and growth. This is the third meeting; all subsequent meetings will be closed to newcomers."

"You will find new relationships opening up to you as you spend time with the group and share experiences, strengths and hopes. The quality of these relationships may be unlike any other you have experienced."

"The principal purpose of this workshop is to facilitate healing and recovery. You will be asked to do some unfamiliar things, such as; trusting others, practicing healthy dependence and interdependence, listening carefully and sharing your feelings. You will have the opportunity to experience what life within a healthy can be."

7:25 [Allow approximately 20 minutes for the following.]

"In a few minutes, I am going to pass out the ***Participation Agreement.*** This agreement establishes the guidelines we will use during this workshop. The effectiveness of this program and the success of those individuals who preceded you form the basis for this agreement. Accepting them is your choice. The level of your success will depend upon your desire to be supportive to others working the program and your willingness to abide by the agreement. Take the agreement with you this evening and bring it next week."

"Families are selected at random by dividing the name cards equally into groups. This procedure may sound controlling, but it has been proven to be a safe and 'nonjudgmental' approach to 'family group' selection. It is a big step toward 'letting go'."

[Ask for small groups of four to six people to be formed, depending on the total group size.]

[Refer to *Participation Agreement* in Appendix Two.]

[Read the *Participation Agreement,* using the *Facilitator's Script* in Appendix Two as a guideline.]

[Have a copy of the *Participation Agreement* and *Week #3* writing exercise available for those who do not have the workbook.]

[Pass out 3x5 note cards and ask each individual to complete the card, listing their first name, last initial and telephone number. These cards will be used to form family groups and create a group roster prior to the next meeting.]

7:45 [Allow approximately 10 minutes for writing.]

[Prior to start of writing exercise]:

(If available, soft music is useful during the writing segment)

"Ten minutes are allowed to complete the individual writing process. I will give a three-minute warning to allow you to complete your writing."

7:55 [Allow approximately 25 minutes for the following.]

[End of writing time]:

"Sharing your writing work within each group will last twenty-five minutes. Focus on your writing and allow everyone to share, answering one question at a time. Until everyone has shared, please don't crosstalk. "Crosstalk" is when two people enter into a dialogue that excludes other group members. Please limit your comments or observations to your own personal experience. I'll give a three-minute warning to allow you to complete the sharing."

"Try not to 'intellectualize' when sharing. To the best of your ability, share the feelings you experienced while writing (e.g., joy, sadness, anger, love, guilt, hurt, loneliness).

8:20 [Allow approximately 30 minutes for the following.]

[End of small group sharing]:

"Please rearrange your chairs into one large circle. The meeting is now open for sharing tonight's experiences."

8:50 [Allow 10 minutes to conclude the meeting.]

[End of large group sharing]:

"The material that will be used from the workbook each week will guide you through the writing processes dealing with each Step. It is not intended to provide all the possible information on each Step or Bible citation."

[Ask for any announcements.]

"Reminder! What you hear at this meeting is confidential; please leave it at this meeting! It is not for public disclosure or gossip. Please respect the privacy of those who shared here tonight."

"Will everyone please clean up after themselves and help re-arrange the room?"

"Please join me in a closing prayer, followed by the Lord's Prayer."

9:00 [Adjourn.]

MEETING PREPARATION FOR WEEK 4

- **Assign family groups by sorting the 3x5 cards randomly into family groups.**
- **Prepare a group roster of all participants, divided into family groups. The list is to include first name, last initial and telephone number.**
- **Have copies of the group roster available to distribute.**
- **If possible, participants who have indicated a desire to be in an exclusively female or male group should be in one group.**

FACILITATOR'S SCRIPT

STEP STUDY WRITING WORKSHOP PARTICIPATION AGREEMENT

Secretary: When reviewing the **Participation Agreement,** it is helpful to use this work sheet in order to expand the explanation and emphasize the value of the **Participation Agreement.**

Give my maximum effort by actively participating in weekly meetings and maintaining contact with my Step Study family members between meetings.

- Steps One, Two and Three are the foundation Steps.
  - They build inner strength and encourage the development of our capacity to rely on our relationship with Jesus Christ.
  - Violation of Steps Two and Three is often the basis for further trouble and confusion.
- In choosing health and recovery, we must be prepared to discover that:
  - Our journey will frequently be painful as a result of changes that take place.
  - Our new patterns and habits may frequently bring condemnation from others who are confounded by our changed behavior.
  - Electing to seek a new life may appear abnormal, since our dysfunctional behavior has been seen as "normal" by us and many people around us.

Be as confident as possible, relying on God for help and healing.

- God is committed to using imperfection to achieve His purposes for His children.
- We are all equal recipients of the Love of God we receive through Jesus Christ.
- We will acknowledge our humanity by working Step One to the utmost of our ability. Remember, only God's Holy Spirit does the healing in all our lives. To be available for healing we need to:
  - Work the Steps consistently.
  - Pray for healing, recovery and miracles.
- Our intention in this workshop is to develop skills and relationships that will enhance our ability to:
  - Nurture and parent ourselves.
  - Create a network of support for ourselves and others.

Support my family group by giving each person my undivided attention.

- To support each other in nurturing, ministering and healing we must:
  - Not interrupt.
  - Be genuinely there. We give support through example.
  - Realize that God's Holy Spirit works through us to enable us to break through barriers.
  - Suspend judgment or evaluation of progress.
  - Not support others when they choose to ignore or refuse to deal with their problems.

Be as honest as possible in all things.
  - Telling the truth, as we know it, may be a new experience for us.
  - Denial is confronted when we are honest with others and ourselves.

Openly share my uncomfortable feelings when someone makes offensive comments or uses inappropriate language.

- By honestly acknowledging how we experience another person's communication, we respect our individual needs.
  - We do not have to accept verbal abuse.
  - We do not have to remain in the presence of anyone who is using language that offends us.

Humbly submit to the process and do my best to suspend negative judgment.

- Regardless of how we feel, do as much of the work as is possible.
- The format of this workshop includes structure and writing as regular parts of the process. The procedures used are directly related to the purpose intended.
- The major differences between this workshop and other Twelve Step groups are:
  - The commitment to write; this is a critically important part of the workshop. It is important to follow the directions whether or not we agree with them.
  - The lack of focus on emotional support alone. If this is the only need, other options are available, such as seeing a trained counselor or therapist.

Schedule time between weekly meetings to complete the written work on the Step and to study the Step as thoroughly as possible.

- Having family group meetings before the regular workshop time may allow for interaction that the workshop does not provide. Each family group will have to assess the need for this as they get to know each other.

- Greater understanding of the healing process can be gained by studying material on inner healing, prayer and the work of the Holy Spirit. See Appendix Seven for a partial list of appropriate supplemental materials.

Accept the discomfort and unsettling behavior changes that may accompany working the Twelve Steps.

- Avoid the common mistake made during the process of recovery: that is, resorting to addictive, compulsive or obsessive behavior to distract from the pain.

- To make the greatest progress in working the Steps, it is best to refrain from developing a new intimate or sexual relationship. Such a focus can detract from our commitment to recovery.

- Friendships can and will develop from this Program. Rely on these new relationships for support in experiencing the utmost from the Step work.

Keep my commitment to myself and to my family group by regularly attending the weekly meetings.

- Schedule other activities around meetings.
  - Only an emergency is a bona-fide excuse for nonattendance.

- Harmony and results in this Step Study will be enhanced if family group members interact and communicate with one another between meetings.

Share my experience, strength and hope during the meeting.

- We demonstrate support by:
  - Not giving advice.
  - Taking responsibility for ourselves, rather than trying to fix others.
  - Being honest.
  - Withholding judgment. It is not helpful to point out what's wrong with another person's behavior.

- People will get what they need either in the meeting or in their daily lives; we are not responsible for providing their needs.

Refrain from trying to "explain" situations when sharing, and do my best to clearly identify and share my feelings (e.g., joy, sadness, depression, anger, love, hate, guilt, loneliness, inadequacy).

- Feelings do not require analysis; they require proper response.

- Pay attention to what our body is saying. Many of us cannot distinguish one sensation from another. As we progress in this work, appropriate labels for feelings will develop.

Incorporate the "Five Practices of Recovery" into my daily life.

- We learn from others, and others learn from us. The most useful arena for sharing recovery experiences is the step study meeting.

- Reading about the Steps fosters understanding; doing the required work in each Step assures results.

- God is always available and patiently waits for us to pray and meditate daily.

- The most immediate way to request support when we need it is to use the telephone. Often, a spontaneous call is an opportunity to acknowledge that we are thinking of someone and appreciate his or her presence in our lives. The telephone works both ways.

- All evidence indicates that we will be confronted daily by our human nature. Our relationship with Christ is strengthened when we can begin and end each day with a review of our work in the first three Steps.

SAMPLE STEP STUDY WRITING WORKSHOP FORMAT
WEEK #4 TO WEEK #28

[Reward promptness by starting the meeting on time.]

7:00 [Allow approximately 15 minutes for the following.]

[Pass out *Milestones in Recovery, The Twelve Steps* and *Scripture for The Twelve Steps.]*

"Will everyone please be seated with their family groups."

"Good evening! Welcome to the _____ Step Study Writing Workshop. My name is _____ , and I am your trusted servant for tonight."

[As the leader, it is your choice whether prayer is silent or aloud.]

"Please join me for a moment of prayer, after which we will recite the Serenity Prayer."

"I have asked _____ to read *Milestones in Recovery.*"

"I have asked _____ to read *The Twelve Steps.*"

"I have asked _____ to read *Scripture for The Twelve Steps* after each step."

"Our tradition is to be self-supporting through our own contributions. We ask for your contribution at this time to avoid interrupting the meeting."

7:15 [Allow approximately 10 minutes for writing.]

[Prior to start of writing exercise]:

(If available, soft music is useful during the writing segment.)

"Ten minutes are allowed to complete for writing, followed by forty-five minutes of family sharing. Then we will all join together."

"The writing and sharing topic for tonight is on Step _____ . Focus on your writing and allow time for everyone to share, answering one question at a time. Until everyone has shared, please do not crosstalk. "Crosstalk" is when two people enter into a dialogue that excludes other group members. Your sharing is most valuable when you limit your comments or observations to your own personal experience. I'll give a three-minute warning to complete the sharing."

[(Start music if available.]

[Give a three-minute warning prior to the end of family writing.]

7:25 [Allow 45 minutes for family group sharing.]

Give a three-minute warning prior to the end of family sharing.]

8:10 [Allow 5 minutes to form the large group.]

[Stop music; announce that it is time to form the large group.]

"Please open the family groups to include everyone."

[When everyone is seated]:

8:15: [Allow 30 minutes for large group sharing.]

"Will everyone please introduce themselves by giving their first name." "During the remaining thirty minutes, please limit your sharing to three minutes so that everyone has an opportunity to share. To begin the sharing, does someone have an answered prayer from their prayer requests, recovery experiences from working the Steps or results from family group interaction during the previous week?"

8:45 [Allow 10 minutes for the following.]

"Does anyone have a prayer request regarding themselves or others?"

"I have asked _____ to lead us in prayer for our requests."

8:55 [Optional.]

"I have asked_____ to read *The Participation Agreement*" on page 156.

"Are there any announcements?"

[See workshop schedule to announce the group leading next week.]

"Family group number_____ is leading the meeting next week."

"Reminder! What you hear at this meeting is confidential; please leave it at this meeting! It is not for public disclosure or gossip. Please respect the privacy of those who shared here tonight. And, do your best to call your family group during this week."

"Will everyone please clean up after themselves and help rearrange the room?"

"Will all who care to, stand and join me in closing with the Lord's Prayer?"

"Keep coming back, it works!"

9:00 [Adjourn.]

SAMPLE MEETING GUIDELINES FOR SECRETARY

These guidelines are to be used by the secretary or the person who is leading the meeting for the evening.

- Before the regular meeting begins, read through the evening's writing exercise that includes material on the Step and Bible scripture.

- Ask each group to phone those who are absent in order to support their next attendance.

- Remind the groups to focus individual sharing on the Step being worked. Encourage recovery-type sharing.

  • Sharing is to be focused on individual experience, strength and hope in working the Steps.

  • It is not necessary for everyone to share.

  • Allow equal time for everyone in the group to share.

- Encourage each group to meet at another time for more opportunities to process writing and to deepen "family group" bonding and trust. An alternative to meeting is telephoning regularly. See Appendix Six for a telephone roster.

- Encourage group members to share outside reading. Emphasize the importance of doing outside reading to broaden one's understanding of the Steps and Bible scripture.

- Be as loving, supportive and positive as possible, recognizing you won't always feel this way.

- Be a good friend who is willing to listen, yet does not give advice.

APPENDIX THREE

COMMON BEHAVIOR CHARACTERISTICS
PROCESSES AND QUESTIONS FOR WEEK #2

● Refer to **Common Behavior Characteristics of Adult Children.** Select the behavior characteristic that best describes you and indicate how it is currently affecting your life.

_____

_____

_____

_____

_____

● What changes would you like to see in your life as a result of working the Steps? _____

_____

_____

_____

_____

● How will your relationship with the Lord support you in accomplishing your goals in recovery? _____

_____

_____

_____

_____

_____

● During the past week, what insights resulted from working the material in the book?

_____

_____

_____

_____

_____

Allocate equal time for each family member. Please limit individual sharing to explanations of the written material. Allow time for contributions from family members after writing has been shared.

INTRODUCTION TO FAMILY GROUP COMMUNICATION, SUPPORT AND RECOVERY

Quality communication among family group members is essential for successful completion of the materials in the step narrative portion and weekly writing exercises. Before you read any further, please take a moment to review what was written about the family group experiences in the Methods of Study in Appendix One.

The **Step Study Writing Workshop** is a method for looking at painful experiences from our past that are continuing to influence our lives today. Writing about and sharing our progress with the Steps involves a process of re-defining our knowledge and understanding of ourselves. As we share our recovery story with our family group, we will discover how our attitudes about ourselves and others are often founded on faulty information. Information has been passed on to us from parents, siblings and other relatives who did not know, or perhaps care to know, the truth about their own worth and value, or the beauty of other people.

As we work through the material in this Step Study, we will begin to see life through the eyes of an adult, rather than the eyes of a terrified, fearful and shame-filled child. We are not in this program to continue to view ourselves as victims. We are here to accept the reality of the past and work to enhance the quality of our present lives through working the Twelve Steps.

We will be sharing the process of our recovery with our family group members. Supporting one another in identifying the fears and resentments of our past will help us break the vicious cycle of passing dysfunctional and addictive behavior on to our own children. If we are not restored to wholeness, our own children may also be faced with maladaptive behavior in their lives.

A challenge often faced by participants working this material is developing a desire and a means to communicate with family group members between weekly meetings. This is an important factor in successful working of the materials in this book. We may be unaccustomed to having people actively interested in improving the quality of our lives. Sharing with family group members offers an opportunity to experience supportive-type relating. Sharing in the weekly meetings and being in contact with family members between meetings is a way to discover new "friends in recovery."

Successful sharing begins with the realization that the members of our family group cannot read our minds. If we find ourselves becoming resentful or angry because others are not responding to our problems, we need to remember that they cannot know or respond to what we don't tell them. If we are reluctant to share because our confidences have been betrayed in the past, this is an opportunity to rebuild our trust. By sharing openly we discover what is in our own hearts and minds. The dynamics of self-revelation (discovering exactly what we feel and think) occur through communicating with other persons. Through the process of sharing, something mysterious, powerful and subtle happens that gives us the courage to shed our fear of discovery. By asking for and receiving the support of others, we are empowered to allow the past to slip away and to develop a new life.

As we write and share the working of this material, our stories may be ones we have told in the past. It is important to view our sharing as re-defining our past behavior, not telling and re-telling the unhappy details of shattered dreams and painful childhood experiences. If our stories are repeated often and dramatically, we may find them being exaggerated as they are retold. We must examine our motives for re-telling the drama of our past. Is it because we feel like victims? Are we blaming others or making excuses? Are we wallowing in our past miseries and re-charging old resentments? Part of our recovery is getting rid of our old behavior. This means taking time to listen carefully to what we are sharing and asking the

(Continued on page 174)

STEP ONE
PROCESSES AND QUESTIONS FOR WEEK #3 (Step 1—Week 1)

We admitted we were powerless over the effects of our separation from God—
that our lives had become unmanageable.

I know nothing good lives in me, that is, in my sinful nature.
For I have the desire to do what is good, but I cannot carry it out. (Romans 7:18)

● What is your main objective in choosing to participate in this workshop? _____

_____

_____

_____

_____

● What anxieties do you have about making a weekly commitment for a six-month period?

_____

_____

_____

_____

● How is Paul's inner struggle (Romans 7:18) similar to yours? _____

_____

_____

_____

_____

_____

● During the past week, what insights resulted from working the material in the book? ___

_____

_____

_____

_____

_____

Allocate equal time for each family member. Please limit individual sharing to explanations of the written material. Allow time for contributions from family members after writing has been shared.

family group members to respond to our communication. If what we are talking about does not support our recovery, there is no reason for sharing it.

Some of us have never overcome the fear of revealing our true feelings. We justify this fear by stating that we have nothing to offer. This is not true, and since the quality of our relationships will be determined by the honesty of our sharing, we must each learn how to open ourselves to others in our family group. This process will post another milestone in the task of breaking the destructive cycle of failure feeding upon failure. By sharing openly, we demonstrate that we trust our family group and willingly agree to be vulnerable to them. Nothing equals the importance of revealing our real selves so we can be known, healed and loved.

This work also prepares us to become mentors to other people who are newly aware of themselves as Adult Children. In this workshop and in other places and times, we demonstrate to others what we are learning for ourselves. We all take turns being followers until we are ready to lead. Those who preceded us enabled us to follow their example as they shared their experience, strength and hope. We learn from others by the principles and practices that produced positive and healthy experiences for them. By our continued commitment to heal our character flaws, we will find others looking to us for comfort, direction and wisdom.

For many of us, our participation in this Step Study makes us want to bring together members of our biological families who may be estranged from us or each other. This is because each of us has a deep desire to participate as loved and loving members of a healthy and whole family system. We may be able to do this successfully with our own families, or we may discover that our real family is made up of people who love us, whether they are relatives or not. During holidays and other family-type celebrations, there will be ample opportunities for us to choose to enjoy the occasion with our "new" family members. We have the choice to connect with either or both families of loved ones who welcome our participation with them. This is clearly a time for us to realize that in our program of recovery, we no longer have to be without a loving family.

STEP ONE
PROCESSES AND QUESTIONS FOR WEEK #4 (Step 1—Week 2)

We admitted we were powerless over the effects of our separation from God—
that our lives had become unmanageable.

I know nothing good lives in me, that is, in my sinful nature.
For I have the desire to do what is good, but I cannot carry it out.   (Romans 7:18)

● List events that occurred during the week that illustrate your powerlessness. _____

_____

_____

_____

_____

_____

● List events that occurred during the week that illustrate the unmanageability of your life.

_____

_____

_____

_____

_____

● What difficulties do you have in being as open about your struggles as Paul was (Romans 7:18)? _____

_____

_____

_____

_____

_____

_____

● During the past week, what insights resulted from working the material in the book? ___

_____

_____

_____

_____

_____

Allocate equal time for each family member. Please limit individual sharing to explanations of the written material. Allow time for contributions from family members after writing has been shared.

FAMILY GROUP CONTACT RECORD
WEEK #5

Date: _____ Person _____ Subject _____

Result of communication and action taken: _____

_____

_____

_____

Feelings experienced (love, anger, pain, support, acknowledgement): _____

_____

_____

_____

Date: _____ Person _____ Subject _____

Result of communication and action taken: _____

_____

_____

_____

Feelings experienced (love, anger, pain, support, acknowledgement): _____

_____

_____

_____

Prayer Requests from family group or step study: _____

_____

_____

_____

_____

Answered Prayers; thanksgiving and comfort received: _____

_____

_____

_____

_____

_____

_____

STEP TWO
PROCESSES AND QUESTIONS FOR WEEK #5 (Step 2—Week 1)
Came to believe that a Power greater than ourselves could restore us to sanity.
For it is God who works in you to will and to act according to his good purpose. (Philippians 2:13)

- As part of tonight's family group sharing, introduce yourself and share your history; be brief, but clear. Also, restate for your family group your main objective in choosing to participate in this workshop. (See Step 1—Week 1 writing exercise.) _____

_____

_____

_____

_____

_____

- What events occurred during the week that demonstrate your irrational behavior? _____

_____

_____

_____

_____

_____

- How does Christ act as your guide in working out your life purpose (Philippians 2:13)?

_____

_____

_____

_____

_____

- During the past week, what insights resulted from working the material in the book? ___

_____

_____

_____

_____

_____

Allocate equal time for each family member. Please limit individual sharing to explanations of the written material. Allow time for contributions from family members after writing has been shared.

177

FAMILY GROUP CONTACT RECORD
WEEK #6

Date: _____ Person _____ Subject _____

Result of communication and action taken: _____

_____

_____

_____

Feelings experienced (love, anger, pain, support, acknowledgement): _____

_____

_____

_____

Prayer Requests from family group or step study: _____

_____

_____

_____

Answered Prayers; thanksgiving and comfort received: _____

_____

_____

_____

A WORD ABOUT LEAVING YOUR FAMILY GROUP

Most of us are free to do as we please. When we want to go, we go; when we want to stay, we stay. Participating with your family group has possibly raised some questions as to the compatibility of your family members and made you feel like you didn't want to stay with your family. If you are experiencing pain, frustration or discomfort from working the Step material, you may feel discouraged and fearful. You may have fallen behind, and are finding it difficult to complete the work. If you have not developed a close bond with your family members, you may consider quitting.

If any of these feelings and thoughts are present, we strongly suggest that you:

1. Take a risk; reach out to your family group (or an individual member), and share your true feelings and fears.

2. Take time to consider the options; ask for help from the Lord, and make the decision which will be best for you.

When you make your final decision, inform your family members. Allow them to preserve the dignity of their experience. Do not be concerned about their reaction. It is important for you to become able to express your needs and wants, and realize that other people are there to be supportive. This is a healthy way to complete the relationship, and will help to minimize any feelings of abandonment which may result from your decision to leave.

STEP TWO
PROCESSES AND QUESTIONS FOR WEEK #6 (Step 2—Week 2)

Came to believe that a Power greater than ourselves could restore us to sanity.

For it is God who works in you to will and to act according to his good purpose. (Philippians 2:13)

- Describe your relationship with God during childhood. _____
  _____
  _____
  _____
  _____
  _____

- What events in your life interfere with your relationship with God? _____
  _____
  _____
  _____
  _____
  _____

- What difficulties do you have in accepting that God's power working in you can restore you to sanity (Philippians 2:13)? _____
  _____
  _____
  _____
  _____
  _____

- During the past week, what insights resulted from working the material in the book? ___
  _____
  _____
  _____
  _____
  _____

Allocate equal time for each family member. Please limit individual sharing to explanations of the written material. Allow time for contributions from family members after writing has been shared.

FAMILY GROUP CONTACT RECORD
WEEK #7

Date: _____ Person _____ Subject _____

Result of communication and action taken: _____

_____

_____

_____

Feelings experienced (love, anger, pain, support, acknowledgement): _____

_____

_____

_____

Date: _____ Person _____ Subject _____

Result of communication and action taken: _____

_____

_____

_____

Feelings experienced (love, anger, pain, support, acknowledgement): _____

_____

_____

_____

Prayer Requests from family group or step study: _____

_____

_____

_____

_____

Answered Prayers; thanksgiving and comfort received: _____

_____

_____

_____

_____

_____

STEP THREE
PROCESSES AND QUESTIONS FOR WEEK #7 (Step 3—Week 1)

Made a decision to turn our will and our lives over to the care of God as we understood Him.

Therefore, I urge you, brothers, in view of God's mercy, to offer your bodies as living sacrifices, holy and pleasing to God—which is your spiritual worship. (Romans 12:1)

● What areas in your life need to be turned over to God? Explain. _____
_____
_____
_____
_____
_____

● What outcome do you expect in turning your life over to God's care? _____
_____
_____
_____
_____
_____

● What is your interpretation of Romans 12:1 as it relates to Step Three? _____
_____
_____
_____
_____
_____

● During the past week, what insights resulted from working the material in the book? __
_____
_____
_____
_____
_____

Allocate equal time for each family member. Please limit individual sharing to explanations of the written material. Allow time for contributions from family members after writing has been shared.

FAMILY GROUP CONTACT RECORD
WEEK #8

Date: _____ Person _____ Subject _____

Result of communication and action taken: _____

_____

_____

_____

Feelings experienced (love, anger, pain, support, acknowledgement): _____

_____

_____

_____

Date: _____ Person _____ Subject _____

Result of communication and action taken: _____

_____

_____

_____

Feelings experienced (love, anger, pain, support, acknowledgement): _____

_____

_____

Prayer Requests from family group or step study: _____

_____

_____

_____

_____

Answered Prayers; thanksgiving and comfort received: _____

_____

_____

_____

_____

STEP THREE
PROCESSES AND QUESTIONS FOR WEEK #8 (Step 3—Week 2)

Made a decision to turn our will and our lives over to the care of God as we understood Him.

Therefore, I urge you, brothers, in view of God's mercy, to offer your bodies as living sacrifices, holy and pleasing to God—which is your spiritual worship. (Romans 12:1)

• Describe situations where self-will has interfered with your decision to turn your will over to God's care.

_____

_____

_____

_____

_____

• Cite situations during the week in which you successfully worked Step Three. _____

_____

_____

_____

_____

_____

• In Romans 12:2, Paul instructs: *"Do not conform any longer to the pattern of this world, but be transformed by the renewing of your mind. Then you will be able to test and approve what God's will is—his good, pleasing and perfect will."* How do you conform to the world? _____

_____

_____

_____

_____

• During the past week, what insights resulted from working the material in the book? ___

_____

_____

_____

_____

Allocate equal time for each family member. Please limit individual sharing to explanations of the written material. Allow time for contributions from family members after writing has been shared.

FAMILY GROUP CONTACT RECORD
WEEK #9

Date: _____ Person _____ Subject _____

Result of communication and action taken: _____

_____

_____

_____

Feelings experienced (love, anger, pain, support, acknowledgement): _____

_____

_____

_____

Date: _____ Person _____ Subject _____

Result of communication and action taken: _____

_____

_____

_____

Feelings experienced (love, anger, pain, support, acknowledgement): _____

_____

_____

_____

Prayer Requests from family group or step study: _____

_____

_____

_____

_____

Answered Prayers; thanksgiving and comfort received: _____

_____

_____

_____

_____

Week #10 exercise focuses on the *Resentment* and *Fear Exercises*. When doing your inventory, start with the traits you are most familiar with. This will help you develop a comfortable way in which to prepare your inventory.

STEP FOUR
PROCESSES AND QUESTIONS FOR WEEK #9 (Step 4—Week 1)

Made a searching and fearless moral inventory of ourselves.

Let us examine our ways and test them, and let us return to the Lord. (Lamentations 3:40)

- In what areas of your life are you using denial or rationalization? _____

  _____

  _____

  _____

  _____

  _____

- What kind of support do you want from your family group to help you complete Step Four (e.g., telephone support, meeting outside of regular meetings)? Please ask for what you want. No one can read your mind. _____

  _____

  _____

  _____

  _____

  _____

- Why do we return to the Lord after a thorough self-examination (Lamentations 3:40)?

  _____

  _____

  _____

  _____

  _____

  _____

- During the past week, what insights resulted from working the material in the book? ___

  _____

  _____

  _____

  _____

  _____

Allocate equal time for each family member. Please limit individual sharing to explanations of the written material. Allow time for contributions from family members after writing has been shared.

FAMILY GROUP CONTACT RECORD
WEEK #10

Date: _____ Person _____ Subject _____

Result of communication and action taken: _____

_____

_____

_____

Feelings experienced (love, anger, pain, support, acknowledgement): _____

_____

_____

_____

Date: _____ Person _____ Subject _____

Result of communication and action taken: _____

_____

_____

_____

Feelings experienced (love, anger, pain, support, acknowledgement): _____

_____

_____

_____

Prayer Requests from family group or step study: _____

_____

_____

_____

_____

Answered Prayers; thanksgiving and comfort received: _____

_____

_____

_____

_____

_____

STEP FOUR
PROCESSES AND QUESTIONS FOR WEEK #10 (Step 4—Week 2)

Made a searching and fearless moral inventory of ourselves.

Let us examine our ways and test them, and let us return to the Lord.   (Lamentations 3:40)

- Briefly describe your progress in preparing for your Step Four inventory. List any difficulties that you are having. _____

  _____

  _____

  _____

  _____

  _____

- Discuss your main resentment and your main fear. Refer to the **Resentment** and **Fear Exercises** if necessary. _____

  _____

  _____

  _____

  _____

  _____

  _____

- How will you return to the Lord if you have strayed (Lamentations 3:40)? _____

  _____

  _____

  _____

  _____

  _____

- During the past week, what insights resulted from working the material in the book? ___

  _____

  _____

  _____

  _____

  _____

Allocate equal time for each family member. Please limit individual sharing to explanations of the written material. Allow time for contributions from family members after writing has been shared.

FAMILY GROUP CONTACT RECORD
WEEK #11

Date: _____ Person _____ Subject _____

Result of communication and action taken: _____

_____

_____

_____

Feelings experienced (love, anger, pain, support, acknowledgement): _____

_____

_____

_____

Date: _____ Person _____ Subject _____

Result of communication and action taken: _____

_____

_____

_____

Feelings experienced (love, anger, pain, support, acknowledgement): _____

_____

_____

_____

Prayer Requests from family group or step study: _____

_____

_____

_____

_____

Answered Prayers; thanksgiving and comfort received: _____

_____

_____

_____

_____

_____

STEP FOUR
PROCESSES AND QUESTIONS FOR WEEK #11 (Step 4—Week 3)

Made a searching and fearless moral inventory of ourselves.

Let us examine our ways and test them, and let us return to the Lord.   (Lamentations 3:40)

- How will your Fourth Step inventory clear the way to a deeper relationship with Christ? __

  _____
  _____
  _____
  _____
  _____
  _____

- As you deepen your relationship with God, which one of your "strengths" provides the most benefits and rewards? _____

  _____
  _____
  _____
  _____
  _____
  _____

- Matthew 26:41 tells us: *"Watch and pray so that you will not fall into temptation. The spirit is willing, but the body is weak."* Which one of your "weaknesses" gives you the most difficulty? _

  _____
  _____
  _____
  _____
  _____

- During the past week, what insights resulted from working the material in the book? __

  _____
  _____
  _____
  _____
  _____

Allocate equal time for each family member. Please limit individual sharing to explanations of the written material. Allow time for contributions from family members after writing has been shared.

FAMILY GROUP CONTACT RECORD
WEEK #12

Date: _____ Person _____ Subject _____

Result of communication and action taken: _____

_____

_____

_____

Feelings experienced (love, anger, pain, support, acknowledgement): _____

_____

_____

_____

Date: _____ Person _____ Subject _____

Result of communication and action taken: _____

_____

_____

_____

Feelings experienced (love, anger, pain, support, acknowledgement): _____

_____

_____

_____

Prayer Requests from family group or step study: _____

_____

_____

_____

_____

Answered Prayers; thanksgiving and comfort received: _____

_____

_____

_____

_____

Week #13 exercise focuses on the *Guidelines For Preparing Your Fifth Step*.

STEP FIVE
PROCESSES AND QUESTIONS FOR WEEK #12 (Step 5—Week 1)
Admitted to God, to ourselves, and to another human being the exact nature of our wrongs.
Therefore confess your sins to each other and pray for each other
so that you may be healed.   (James 5:16a)

- Proverbs 28:13 tells us: *"He who conceals his sins does not prosper, but whoever confesses and renounces them finds mercy."* How does concealing your sins hinder your progress in working the Steps? _____

  _____

  _____

  _____

- How do you feel toward the members of your family group? _____

  _____

  _____

  _____

  _____

- What have you been unwilling to ask from your family group? What are you willing to ask for now? _____

  _____

  _____

  _____

  _____

- What have you been unwilling to give to your family group? What are you willing to give to them now? _____

  _____

  _____

  _____

  _____

- During the past week, what insights resulted from working the material in the book? ___

  _____

  _____

  _____

  _____

Allocate equal time for each family member. Please limit individual sharing to explanations of the written material. Allow time for contributions from family members after writing has been shared.

FAMILY GROUP CONTACT RECORD
WEEK #13

Date: _____ Person _____ Subject _____
Result of communication and action taken: _____
_____
_____
_____

Feelings experienced (love, anger, pain, support, acknowledgement): _____
_____
_____
_____

Date: _____ Person _____ Subject _____
Result of communication and action taken: _____
_____
_____
_____

Feelings experienced (love, anger, pain, support, acknowledgement): _____
_____
_____
_____

Prayer Requests from family group or step study: _____
_____
_____
_____
_____

Answered Prayers; thanksgiving and comfort received: _____
_____
_____
_____
_____

Week #14 is an opportunity to plan a break for the Step Study participants. See Week #14 for suggestions.

STEP FIVE
PROCESSES AND QUESTIONS FOR WEEK #13 (Step 5—Week 2)

Admitted to God, to ourselves, and to another human being the exact nature of our wrongs.

Therefore confess your sins to each other and pray for each other
so that you may be healed. (James 5:16a)

- Review the **Guidelines For Preparing Your Fifth Step.** Describe how you plan to complete your Fifth Step. _____

  _____

  _____

  _____

  _____

  _____

- Reflecting on James 5:16, what do you need to inspire your personal growth? How can your Step Study family group help? _____

  _____

  _____

  _____

  _____

  _____

- During the past week, what insights resulted from working the material in the book? ___

  _____

  _____

  _____

  _____

  _____

SPECIAL NOTE:
During your family group sharing, separate into pairs and share some part of your Fifth Step with your partner. This exercise will help you complete your Fifth Step with another person. As part of tonight's sharing, discuss your experience of this interaction.

Allocate equal time for each family member. Please limit individual sharing to explanations of the written material. Allow time for contributions from family members after writing has been shared.

FAMILY GROUP CONTACT RECORD
WEEK #14

Date: _____ Person _____ Subject _____

Result of communication and action taken: _____

_____

_____

_____

_____

Feelings experienced (love, anger, pain, support, acknowledgement): _____

_____

_____

_____

Date: _____ Person _____ Subject _____

Result of communication and action taken: _____

_____

_____

_____

Feelings experienced (love, anger, pain, support, acknowledgement): _____

_____

_____

_____

Prayer Requests from family group or step study: _____

_____

_____

_____

_____

Answered Prayers; thanksgiving and comfort received: _____

_____

_____

_____

_____

WEEK #14

SUGGESTIONS RELATIVE TO A STEP STUDY GROUP BREAK

At this point in the Step Study process, it has proven helpful to use one of the meetings following Step Five to plan a break from the regular Step Study routine. Having spent five or more weeks on Steps Four and Five, participants are oftentimes overwhelmed by their experiences. Some of them are behind in their writing and need time to catch up. This break is an opportunity for all the family groups to engage in an activity which is relaxing and allows time to socialize outside the regular Step Study meeting.

Some suggestions are:

■ Plan an evening out; dinner in a restaurant with a relaxing atmosphere or one with a "childlike", playful environment.

■ Plan a pot luck dinner (depending on the time of year) which can be held outdoors in a restful, relaxed location.

■ Plan a progressive dinner party; have different courses assigned to each "family group."

■ Use the meeting time to play games (e.g. children's games, charades, non-competitive games).

■ Use the meeting time to go to a movie, or rent a movie and have a pot luck dinner at the meeting place.

■ Spend the evening at an amusement park, cook out at the beach or park, or at a video game facility.

■ Plan a birthday party for the "kids" who missed out when growing up.

FAMILY GROUP CONTACT RECORD
WEEK #15

Date: _____ Person _____ Subject _____

Result of communication and action taken: _____

_____

_____

_____

Feelings experienced (love, anger, pain, support, acknowledgement): _____

_____

_____

_____

Date: _____ Person _____ Subject _____

Result of communication and action taken: _____

_____

_____

_____

Feelings experienced (love, anger, pain, support, acknowledgement): _____

_____

_____

_____

Prayer Requests from family group or step study: _____

_____

_____

_____

_____

Answered Prayers; thanksgiving and comfort received: _____

_____

_____

_____

_____

STEP SIX
PROCESSES AND QUESTIONS FOR WEEK #15 (Step 6—Week 1)

Were entirely ready to have God remove all these defects of character.

Humble yourselves before the Lord, and he will lift you up.   (James 4:10)

"BROKEN DREAMS"

As children bring their broken toys
with tears for us to mend,
I brought my broken dreams to God
because He was my friend.
But then, instead of leaving Him
in peace to work alone,
I hung around and tried to help
with ways that were my own.
At last, I snatched them back and cried,
"How can you be so slow?"

"My child," he said,
"What could I do?"
"You never did let go."
Author unknown

● How does the **Broken Dreams Prayer** remind you of your unwillingness to "let go?" ___

_____

_____

_____

_____

_____

● How submissive to God are you? How could you submit to God more effectively this week (James 4:10)? _____

_____

_____

_____

_____

● During the past week, what insights resulted from working the material in the book? ___

_____

_____

_____

_____

Allocate equal time for each family member. Please limit individual sharing to explanations of the written material. Allow time for contributions from family members after writing has been shared.

FAMILY GROUP CONTACT RECORD
WEEK #16

Date: _____ Person _____ Subject _____

Result of communication and action taken: _____

_____

_____

_____

Feelings experienced (love, anger, pain, support, acknowledgement): _____

_____

_____

_____

Date: _____ Person _____ Subject _____

Result of communication and action taken: _____

_____

_____

_____

Feelings experienced (love, anger, pain, support, acknowledgement): _____

_____

_____

_____

Prayer Requests from family group or step study: _____

_____

_____

_____

_____

Answered Prayers; thanksgiving and comfort received: _____

_____

_____

_____

_____

STEP SEVEN
PROCESSES AND QUESTIONS FOR WEEK #16 (Step 7—Week 1)
Humbly asked Him to remove our shortcomings.

If we confess our sins, he is faithful and just and will forgive us our sins
and purify us from all unrighteousness. (1 John 1:9)

"PARADOXES OF PRAYER"

I asked God for strength, that I might achieve
I was made weak, that I might learn humbly to obey…
I asked for health, that I might do greater things
I was given infirmity, that I might to better things…
I asked for riches, that I might be happy
I was given poverty, that I might be wise…
I asked for power, that I might have the praise of men
I was given weakness, that I might feel the need of God…
I asked for all things, that I might enjoy life
I was given life, that I might enjoy all things…
I got nothing that I asked for—but everything I had hoped for

Almost despite myself, my unspoken prayers were answered
I am, among all, most richly blessed!
©Universal Press Syndicate

● How does the **Paradoxes of Prayer** reflect your experiences with prayer?_____
_____
_____
_____
_____

● How do you feel when you confess your sins to God (1 John 1:9)? _____
_____
_____
_____
_____

● During the past week, what insights resulted from working the material in the book? ___
_____
_____
_____
_____
_____

Allocate equal time for each family member. Please limit individual sharing to explanations of
the written material. Allow time for contributions from family members after writing has been
shared.

FAMILY GROUP CONTACT RECORD
WEEK #17

Date: _____ Person _____ Subject _____

Result of communication and action taken: _____

_____

_____

_____

Feelings experienced (love, anger, pain, support, acknowledgement): _____

_____

_____

_____

Date: _____ Person _____ Subject _____

Result of communication and action taken: _____

_____

_____

_____

Feelings experienced (love, anger, pain, support, acknowledgement): _____

_____

_____

_____

Prayer Requests from family group or step study: _____

_____

_____

_____

_____

Answered Prayers; thanksgiving and comfort received: _____

_____

_____

_____

_____

STEP EIGHT
PROCESSES AND QUESTIONS FOR WEEK #17 (Step 8—Week 1)

Made a list of all persons we had harmed, and became willing to make amends to them all.

Do to others as you would have them do to you. (Luke 6:31)

- Name a person to whom you have caused harm. What behavior caused the injury? _____

- What effect did your behavior have on others? _____

- What effect did your behavior have on you? _____

- Why and how do you see yourself as an important name on your amends list? _____

- Cite a situation in which you "did to others as you would have them do to you" (Luke 6:31). _____

- During the past week, what insights resulted from working the material in the book? ___

Allocate equal time for each family member. Please limit individual sharing to explanations of the written material. Allow time for contributions from family members after writing has been shared.

FAMILY GROUP CONTACT RECORD
WEEK #18

Date: _____ Person _____ Subject _____

Result of communication and action taken: _____

_____

_____

_____

Feelings experienced (love, anger, pain, support, acknowledgement): _____

_____

_____

_____

Date: _____ Person _____ Subject _____

Result of communication and action taken: _____

_____

_____

_____

Feelings experienced (love, anger, pain, support, acknowledgement): _____

_____

_____

_____

Prayer Requests from family group or step study: _____

_____

_____

_____

_____

Answered Prayers; thanksgiving and comfort received: _____

_____

_____

_____

_____

Week #19 exercise focuses on the *Amends to Others Exercise*.

STEP EIGHT
PROCESSES AND QUESTIONS FOR WEEK #18 (Step 8—Week 2)

Made a list of all persons we had harmed, and became willing to make amends to them all.

Do to others as you would have them do to you.   (Luke 6:31)

Following are three of the fifteen "Traits of a Healthy Family", as described by Dolores Curran in her book under the same title.

Communication (Trait #1): The "healthy" family communicates and listens.

Affirming and Supporting (Trait #2): The "healthy" family affirms and supports one another.

Getting Help (Trait #15): The "healthy" family admits to, and seeks help with, problems.

- What contact did you make with your Step Study family last week as part of being supported in making your amends list? Describe your experience of the communication. __

_____

_____

_____

_____

- Share with your Step Study family group your perception of the degree of openness in communication within your family group. Also, share your progress with Step Eight. __

_____

_____

_____

_____

- In Philippians 2:14, we are instructed: *"Do everything without complaining or arguing..."* Describe your hesitation in developing your amends list. _____

_____

_____

_____

_____

- During the past week, what insights resulted from working the material in the book? __

_____

_____

_____

_____

Allocate equal time for each family member. Please limit individual sharing to explanations of the written material. Allow time for contributions from family members after writing has been shared.

FAMILY GROUP CONTACT RECORD
WEEK #19

Date: _____ Person _____ Subject _____

Result of communication and action taken: _____

_____

_____

_____

Feelings experienced (love, anger, pain, support, acknowledgement): _____

_____

_____

_____

Date: _____ Person _____ Subject _____

Result of communication and action taken: _____

_____

_____

_____

Feelings experienced (love, anger, pain, support, acknowledgement): _____

_____

_____

_____

Prayer Requests from family group or step study: _____

_____

_____

_____

_____

Answered Prayers; thanksgiving and comfort received: _____

_____

_____

_____

_____

Week #20 exercise focuses on the *Amends to Self Exercise*.

STEP NINE
PROCESSES AND QUESTIONS FOR WEEK #19 (Step 9—Week 1)

Made direct amends to such people wherever possible,
except when to do so would injure them or others.

*Therefore, if you are offering your gift at the altar and there remember that your brother
has something against you, leave your gift there in front of the altar.
First go and be reconciled to your brother; then come and offer your gift.*   (Matthew 5:23-24)

• Select a person to whom an amend is necessary. List the ways in which you would communicate the amend (See **Amends to Others Exercise**). _____
_____
_____
_____
_____
_____

• Matthew 5:24 teaches us to become reconciled before we make an offering to God. What does this mean to you? _____
_____
_____
_____
_____
_____

• During the past week, what insights resulted from working the material in the book? __
_____
_____
_____
_____
_____

SPECIAL NOTE:
During your family group sharing, separate into pairs and practice making the above amend with your partner. Pretend that your partner is the person to whom the amend is to be made. As part of tonight's sharing, discuss your experience of this interaction.

Allocate equal time for each family member. Please limit individual sharing to explanations of the written material. Allow time for contributions from family members after writing has been shared.

FAMILY GROUP CONTACT RECORD
WEEK #20

Date: _____ Person _____ Subject _____
Result of communication and action taken: _____
_____
_____
_____

Feelings experienced (love, anger, pain, support, acknowledgement): _____
_____
_____
_____

Date: _____ Person _____ Subject _____
Result of communication and action taken: _____
_____
_____
_____

Feelings experienced (love, anger, pain, support, acknowledgement): _____
_____
_____
_____

Prayer Requests from family group or step study: _____
_____
_____
_____
_____

Answered Prayers; thanksgiving and comfort received: _____
_____
_____
_____
_____

Week #21 exercise focuses on the *Daily Inventory Log*.

STEP NINE
PROCESSES AND QUESTIONS FOR WEEK #20 (Step 9—Week 2)
Made direct amends to such people wherever possible,
except when to do so would injure them or others.

Therefore, if you are offering your gift at the altar and there remember that your brother
has something against you, leave your gift there in front of the altar.
First go and be reconciled to your brother; then come and offer your gift. (Matthew 5:23-24)

• List some highlights of the amends letter to yourself (See **Amends to Self Exercise**). ____

_____

_____

_____

_____

_____

• Romans 12:18 instructs us: *"If it is possible, as far as it depends on you, live at peace with*
everyone." What does this mean to you? _____

_____

_____

_____

_____

_____

• During the past week, what insights resulted from working the material in the book? ___

_____

_____

_____

_____

_____

SPECIAL NOTE:
During your family group sharing, separate into pairs and practice making the above amend
with your partner. Pretend that your partner is you. As part of tonight's sharing, discuss your
experience of this interaction.

Allocate equal time for each family member. Please limit individual sharing to explanations of
the written material. Allow time for contributions from family members after writing has been
shared.

FAMILY GROUP CONTACT RECORD
WEEK #21

Date: _____ Person _____ Subject _____
Result of communication and action taken: _____
_____
_____
_____

Feelings experienced (love, anger, pain, support, acknowledgement): _____
_____
_____
_____

Date: _____ Person _____ Subject _____
Result of communication and action taken: _____
_____
_____
_____

Feelings experienced (love, anger, pain, support, acknowledgement): _____
_____
_____
_____

Prayer Requests from family group or step study: _____
_____
_____
_____
_____

Answered Prayers; thanksgiving and comfort received: _____
_____
_____
_____
_____

STEP TEN
PROCESSES AND QUESTIONS FOR WEEK #21 (Step 10 — Week 1)

Continued to take personal inventory and, when we were wrong, promptly admitted it.

So, if you think you are standing firm, be careful that you don't fall. (1 Corinthians 10:12)

● Review your actions of last week as recorded on your **Daily Inventory Log.** In what area did you perform well? In what area did you perform poorly? _____

_____

_____

_____

_____

_____

● List ways in which you sensed God's presence as you successfully faced temptation. _____

_____

_____

_____

_____

● Cite a situation in which you thought you were standing firm, but fell (1 Corinthians 10:12). Describe your experience of seeing this in your personal inventory and promptly admitting your wrong. _____

_____

_____

_____

_____

● During the past week, what insights resulted from working the material in the book? ____

_____

_____

_____

_____

Allocate equal time for each family member. Please limit individual sharing to explanations of the written material. Allow time for contributions from family members after writing has been shared.

FAMILY GROUP CONTACT RECORD
WEEK #22

Date: _____ Person _____ Subject _____

Result of communication and action taken: _____

_____

_____

_____

Feelings experienced (love, anger, pain, support, acknowledgement): _____

_____

_____

_____

Date: _____ Person _____ Subject _____

Result of communication and action taken: _____

_____

_____

_____

Feelings experienced (love, anger, pain, support, acknowledgement): _____

_____

_____

_____

Prayer Requests from family group or step study: _____

_____

_____

_____

_____

Answered Prayers; thanksgiving and comfort received: _____

_____

_____

_____

_____

STEP TEN
PROCESSES AND QUESTIONS FOR WEEK #22 (Step 10—Week 2)

Continued to take personal inventory and, when we were wrong, promptly admitted it.

So, if you think you are standing firm, be careful that you don't fall. (1 Corinthians 10:12)

● Review today's thoughts, words and actions. Describe incidents in which you expressed:

Selfishness _____

_____

_____

Dishonesty _____

_____

_____

Anger _____

_____

_____

Fear _____

_____

_____

● Review today's thoughts, words and actions. Describe incidents in which you expressed:

Generosity _____

_____

_____

Honesty _____

_____

_____

Calmness _____

_____

_____

Courage _____

_____

_____

● During the past week, what insights resulted from working the material in the book? ___

_____

_____

Allocate equal time for each family member. Please limit individual sharing to explanations of the written material. Allow time for contributions from family members after writing has been shared.

FAMILY GROUP CONTACT RECORD
WEEK #23

Date: _____ Person _____ Subject _____

Result of communication and action taken: _____

_____

_____

_____

Feelings experienced (love, anger, pain, support, acknowledgement): _____

_____

_____

_____

Date: _____ Person _____ Subject _____

Result of communication and action taken: _____

_____

_____

_____

Feelings experienced (love, anger, pain, support, acknowledgement): _____

_____

_____

_____

Prayer Requests from family group or step study: _____

_____

_____

_____

_____

Answered Prayers; thanksgiving and comfort received: _____

_____

_____

_____

_____

_____

STEP ELEVEN
PROCESSES AND QUESTIONS FOR WEEK #23 (Step 11—Week 1)

Sought through prayer and meditation to improve our conscious contact
with God as we understood Him, praying only for knowledge of His will for us
and the power to carry that out.

Let the word of Christ dwell in you richly. (Colossians 3:16a)

● What thoughts persist that cause you to remain focused on "your will," even while praying for God's guidance? _____

_____

_____

_____

_____

● What methods of prayer and meditation have you found most useful? _____

_____

_____

_____

_____

● Proverbs 16:20 states: *"Whoever gives heed to instruction prospers, and blessed is he who trusts in the Lord."* How does Step Eleven contain a similar message? _____

_____

_____

_____

● During the past week, what insights resulted from working the material in the book? __

_____

_____

_____

_____

Allocate equal time for each family member. Please limit individual sharing to explanations of the written material. Allow time for contributions from family members after writing has been shared.

FAMILY GROUP CONTACT RECORD
WEEK #24

Date: _____ Person _____ Subject _____

Result of communication and action taken: _____

_____

_____

_____

Feelings experienced (love, anger, pain, support, acknowledgement): _____

_____

_____

_____

Date: _____ Person _____ Subject _____

Result of communication and action taken: _____

_____

_____

_____

Feelings experienced (love, anger, pain, support, acknowledgement): _____

_____

_____

_____

Prayer Requests from family group or step study: _____

_____

_____

_____

_____

Answered Prayers; thanksgiving and comfort received: _____

_____

_____

_____

_____

Week #25 is an opportunity to plan a break for the Step Study participants. See week #25 for suggestions.

STEP ELEVEN
PROCESSES AND QUESTIONS FOR WEEK #24 (Step 11—Week 2)

Sought through prayer and meditation to improve our conscious contact
with God as we understood Him, praying only for knowledge of His will for us
and the power to carry that out.

Let the word of Christ dwell in you richly.   (Colossians 3:16a)

"PRAYER OF SAINT FRANCIS OF ASSISI"

Lord, make me an instrument of Your peace!
Where there is hatred—let me sow love
Where there is injury—pardon
Where there is doubt—faith
Where there is despair—hope
Where there is darkness—light
Where there is sadness—joy
O Divine Master, grant that I may not so much seek
To be consoled—as to console
To be loved—as to love
for
It is in giving—that we receive
It is in pardoning—that we are pardoned
It is in dying—that we are born to eternal life.
Amen.

- How does the **Prayer of Saint Francis of Assisi** echo Colossians 3:16? _____
  _____
  _____
  _____
  _____

- Cite an example of your praying only for knowledge of God's will and the power to carry
  it out. What was the outcome? _____
  _____
  _____
  _____
  _____

- During the past week, what insights resulted from working the material in the book? ___
  _____
  _____
  _____

*Allocate equal time for each family member. Please limit individual sharing to explanations of
the written material. Allow time for contributions from family members after writing has been
shared.*

FAMILY GROUP CONTACT RECORD
WEEK #25

Date: _____ Person _____ Subject _____

Result of communication and action taken: _____

_____

_____

_____

Feelings experienced (love, anger, pain, support, acknowledgement): _____

_____

_____

_____

Date: _____ Person _____ Subject _____

Result of communication and action taken: _____

_____

_____

_____

Feelings experienced (love, anger, pain, support, acknowledgement): _____

_____

_____

_____

Prayer Requests from family group or step study: _____

_____

_____

_____

_____

Answered Prayers; thanksgiving and comfort received: _____

_____

_____

_____

_____

_____

Week #26 exercise focuses on the *Twelve Step Exercise*.

WEEK #25

SUGGESTIONS RELATIVE TO A STEP STUDY GROUP BREAK

At this point in the Step Study process, it has proven helpful to use one of the meetings to plan a break from the regular Step Study routine. Some participants are behind in their writing and need time to catch up. This break is an opportunity for all the family groups to engage in an activity which is relaxing and allows time to socialize outside the regular Step Study meeting.

Some suggestions are:

- Plan an evening out; dinner in a restaurant with a relaxing atmosphere or one with a "childlike," playful environment.

- Plan a pot luck dinner (depending on the time of year) which can be held outdoors in a restful, relaxed location.

- Plan a progressive dinner party; have different courses assigned to each "family group."

- Use the meeting time to play games, (e.g. children's games, charades, non-competitive games).

- Use the meeting time to go to a movie, or rent a movie and have a pot luck dinner at the meeting place.

- Spend the evening at an amusement park, at the beach or park, or at a video game facility.

- Plan a birthday party for the "kids" who missed out when growing up.

FAMILY GROUP CONTACT RECORD
WEEK #26

Date: _____ Person _____ Subject _____

Result of communication and action taken: _____

_____

_____

_____

Feelings experienced (love, anger, pain, support, acknowledgement): _____

_____

_____

_____

Date: _____ Person _____ Subject _____

Result of communication and action taken: _____

_____

_____

_____

Feelings experienced (love, anger, pain, support, acknowledgement): _____

_____

_____

_____

Prayer Requests from family group or step study: _____

_____

_____

_____

_____

_____

Answered Prayers; thanksgiving and comfort received: _____

_____

_____

_____

_____

STEP TWELVE
PROCESSES AND QUESTIONS FOR WEEK #26 (Step 12—Week 1)

Having had a spiritual awakening as the result of these steps,
we tried to carry this message to others, and to practice these principles in all our affairs.

*Brothers, if someone is caught in a sin, you who are spiritual should restore him gently.
But watch yourself, or you also may be tempted.* (Galatians 6:1)

- What is the ongoing value of applying the Twelve Steps on a daily basis? _____

  _____

  _____

  _____

  _____

  _____

- How did the **Twelve-Step Exercise** empower you to handle a life situation more effectively? _____

  _____

  _____

  _____

  _____

  _____

- Ecclesiastes 4:10 instructs: *"If one falls down, his friend can help him up. But pity the man who falls and has no one to help him up!"* How does this relate to Step Twelve? _____

  _____

  _____

  _____

  _____

- During the past week, what insights resulted from working the material in the book? ___

  _____

  _____

  _____

  _____

  _____

Allocate equal time for each family member. Please limit individual sharing to explanations of the written material. Allow time for contributions from family members after writing has been shared.

FAMILY GROUP CONTACT RECORD
WEEK #27

Date: _____ Person _____ Subject _____

Result of communication and action taken: _____

_____

_____

_____

Feelings experienced (love, anger, pain, support, acknowledgement): _____

_____

_____

_____

Date: _____ Person _____ Subject _____

Result of communication and action taken: _____

_____

_____

_____

Feelings experienced (love, anger, pain, support, acknowledgement): _____

_____

_____

_____

Prayer Requests from family group or step study: _____

_____

_____

_____

_____

Answered Prayers; thanksgiving and comfort received: _____

_____

_____

_____

_____

STEP TWELVE
PROCESSES AND QUESTIONS FOR WEEK #27 (Step 12—Week 2)
Having had a spiritual awakening as the result of these steps,
we tried to carry this message to others, and to practice these principles in all our affairs.

Brothers, if someone is caught in a sin, you who are spiritual should restore him gently.
But watch yourself, or you also may be tempted. (Galatians 6:1)

This is the final Step Study writing exercise. It is an opportunity for you to acknowledge yourself for having the courage to stay and work with other committed people who are seeking a healthier way of life.

Complete the following statements as you now view your life:

- When I was a child, I _____ .
  _____

- As I grew into adulthood, I _____ .
  _____

- When I became aware of my behavior traits, I _____ .
  _____

  - Having completed the Step Study, I _____ .
  _____

As we may view our lives now, we are the pens through which the ink of our Higher Power flows to write the story of our lives. Our Step work and family group have contributed to our deeper contact with God. Sharing each other's experience, strength and hope has enabled us to expand our faith in our Higher Power and experience unconditional love.

What do you want to say to your family members or the other individuals in the Step Study relative to:

- Your spiritual awakening _____ .
  _____

- Your gratitude for their coaching you _____ .
  _____

- Your commitment to continue working the Steps _____ .
  _____

Allocate equal time for each family member. Please limit individual sharing to explanations of the written material. Allow time for contributions from family members after writing has been shared.

IMPORTANT CLOSING INFORMATION

If the group desires further informal contact, this meeting is an opportunity to schedule a reunion date.

Appendix Four contains a suggested format for the ongoing gathering of those who want to keep actively involved in the Twelve Step process. Important relationships have been formed during this process; further contact with minimal structure can be vital to the continued application of the principles learned in this Step Study.

The importance of continuing to work the Steps has been stressed throughout the narrative of this book. Repeating this experience at an appropriate interval is a valuable way to further the healing work each individual has thus far accomplished.

CLOSING MEETING
PROCESSES AND QUESTIONS FOR WEEK #28

The facilitator(s) for this meeting can use the same time sequence as for family group writing and sharing, ending with all the family groups joining together.

This meeting will complete the work you have done with your family group and the Twelve Steps.

Each person has the opportunity to gently say good-bye with joy, acknowledgement and love. It is most successful if everyone spends the writing time reflecting and writing on the following questions. Saying "thank you" individually and specifically is not necessary. Feelings of gratitude can be communicated within the question responses.

- I want to complete this experience by acknowledging that it has had the following meaning for me: _____

  _____

  _____

- As part of saying goodbye, I want to acknowledge how I feel about this ending. (Feel free to express your present emotional state—it is a healthy part of accepting this change, e.g., loss, sadness, fear, joy, anticipation, gratefulness.) _____

  _____

  _____

GROUP CLOSING PRAYER

This closing prayer is intended to initiate the large group closing prayer. Further statements, covenants, praise and thanksgiving can be offered by each participant.

> "Heavenly Father, I dedicate myself to the love and care of my Higher Power, Jesus Christ. All healing work is carried on with His guidance. I am committed to surrendering all concerns, from the largest to the smallest, to Him. I accept that, with your help, my self-will no longer needs to control my beliefs, thoughts or actions. Each day I give thanks for your Holy Spirit, which is healing my life more deeply. I cooperate with this healing by agreeing to face any pain, knowing you are there. I know that my healing testifies to humanity the power of Your Grace, and is a source of joy and serenity to me. I am ever open for the opportunity to spread the truth and the joy of my recovery, one day at a time."

Personal closing statements to be added to the group prayer:

_____

_____

Allocate equal time for each family member. Please limit individual sharing to explanations of the written material. Allow time for contributions from family members after writing has been shared.

APPENDIX FOUR

SUGGESTED FORMAT FOR AN ONGOING CHRISTIAN STEP STUDY

At the completion of the Step Study Writing Workshop, some group members may want to meet occasionally for support and renewal. It is possible to design a meeting which will fit the time and needs of the individuals involved. Any or all of the following can be utilized in the meeting format.

- **Opening prayer.**

- **Steps and related scripture reading.**

- **Reflection on the meaning of scripture selection.**

- **Personal sharing of experiences.**

- **Personal sharing of problems or areas of concern.**

- **Restatement of mutual commitment to recovery.**

- **Closing prayer.**

Opening Prayer

"Lord Jesus Christ, we give thanks to you for this day, and for the gift of being together. We claim your promise to be with us as we work to be healed and to find your will for our lives. Strengthen us and bless us as we care for ourselves and each other.

Our Father God, we come here to this place to be together as your children, secure in the knowledge that you are enfolding us in your loving presence. Help us as we seek to help each other."
AMEN

Steps and Related Scripture Reading

Choose one or more of the Steps and related scripture for each meeting. See page xiii to select a Step and scripture. Ask someone to read the Step and related scripture aloud.

Reflection on the Meaning of Scripture Selections

Reflection on scripture selection invites communication relating to how the Steps and scripture work to improve one's spiritual life. For example:

- *This Step and scripture has meaning to me and relates to my life because...*
- *The guidance in this Step and scripture can assist my recovery because...*
- *I desire to deepen my understanding of this Step and scriptures, and pattern my mind after the mind of Christ by...*

Personal Sharing of Experiences

Group members can contribute any recent experience with the Steps and other spiritual aids that have nourished their vital union with Christ.

Personal Sharing of Problems or Areas of Concern

Any group member who wishes to share any concerns is encouraged to do so (e.g., regarding family, work or environment).

Restatement of Mutual Commitment to Recovery

"Almighty God, we call upon you to help us as we work to strengthen our will to be healed to wholeness. Hold us through our struggle to set aside our behaviors that would separate us from you. Keep our hearts and minds directed by your will for our full and complete recovery, in the name and for the sake of your son, Jesus Christ, we acknowledge and avow our support for each other."

Prayer requests can be submitted at this point.

Closing Prayers

"Jesus Christ, as we go our separate ways, go with us. Keep us strong and steadfast in our plan for recovery. Help us face temptation with courage and remember your promises of healing to wholeness. Bless our giving and receiving of support from each other. In God's name we pray."

AMEN

"Dear Father God, bless us as we leave this meeting to go back into the world. Be with us and help us be strong and steadfast in our commitment to recovery. Help us share our knowledge and love of Your son Jesus Christ with each other and with all your children. Give us grace and peace."

AMEN

Personal Statements and Affirmations

The following statements and affirmations can be made to a group member either aloud or silently, as an expression of support.

Affirmation

Nothing you have done or will do can separate you from God or from my loving concern. I may not agree with your actions, but I will love you as a person and do all I can to hold you in God's affirming love.

Prayer

I promise to pray for you, believing our caring Father wishes His children to pray for one another, and ask Him for His blessings in your life.

Openness

I promise to strive to become a more open person, disclosing my feelings, my struggles, my joys and my hurts as well as I am able. I will succeed only if I can trust you with my problems and my dreams. I extend my trust to you and affirm your worth to me as a person and a partner in my walk with the Lord.

Confidentiality

I promise to keep whatever is shared within the confines of the group, in order to provide the atmosphere of safety necessary for openness.

Availability

Anything I have—time, energy, insight, etc.—is at your disposal, to the limit of my resources. As part of this availability, I pledge my time on a regular basis, whether in prayer or for an agreed-upon meeting.

Honesty

I agree to tell the truth, so far as I know it, even if it means risking pain for either of us. I will trust our relationship enough to take that risk, realizing that it is in speaking the truth in love that we will find fulfillment in Christ and all things. I will try to express this honesty in a sensitive and loving manner.

Sensitivity

My desire is to be known and understood by you. I commit to extend understanding you and your needs to the best of my ability.

Accountability

I will seek Christ's liberating power through His Holy Spirit and the loving sharing of my supportive friends, so that I might give more of myself to you. I understand that I am accountable only to Christ to become what God has planned for me in His loving creation.

APPENDIX FIVE

FAMILY GROUP TELEPHONE LIST

NAME	TELEPHONE NO. (WORK/TIME)		BEST TIME TO CALL
1. _____	_____	(W)	_____
	_____	(H)	_____
2. _____	_____	(W)	_____
	_____	(H)	_____
3. _____	_____	(W)	_____
	_____	(H)	_____
4. _____	_____	(W)	_____
	_____	(H)	_____
5. _____	_____	(W)	_____
	_____	(H)	_____
6. _____	_____	(W)	_____
	_____	(H)	_____
7. _____	_____	(W)	_____
	_____	(H)	_____

TELEPHONE NUMBERS OF OTHER WORKSHOP PARTICIPANTS

1. _____	_____	(W)	_____
	_____	(H)	_____
2. _____	_____	(W)	_____
	_____	(H)	_____
3. _____	_____	(W)	_____
	_____	(H)	_____
4. _____	_____	(W)	_____
	_____	(H)	_____
5. _____	_____	(W)	_____
	_____	(H)	_____
6. _____	_____	(W)	_____
	_____	(H)	_____
7. _____	_____	(W)	_____
	_____	(H)	_____

APPENDIX SIX
SUGGESTED READING

Alcoholics Anonymous. **The Big Book.** New York, NY: Alcoholics Anonymous World Services, Inc.

Alcoholics Anonymous. **Twelve Steps—Twelve Traditions.** New York, NY: Alcoholics Anonymous World Services, Inc.

Beattie, Melody. **Codependent No More.** New York, NY: Harper and Row Publishers, Inc.

Black, Claudia. **It Will Never Happen To Me.** New York, NY: Ballantine Books.

Bradshaw, John. **Bradshaw on: The Family.** Deerfield Beach, FL: Health Communications, Inc.

Covington, Stephanie & Beckett, Liana. **Leaving The Enchanted Forest: The Path From Relationship Addiction To Intimacy.** New York, NY: Harper & Row.

Fishel, Ruth. **The Journey Within—A Spiritual Path To Recovery.** Deerfield Beach, FL: Health Communications, Inc.

Friel, John and Friel, Linda. **Adult Children—The Secrets of Dysfunctional Families.** Deerfield Beach, FL: Health Communications, Inc.

Friends in Recovery. **The 12 Steps for Adult Children.** San Diego, CA: Recovery Publications.

Friends in Recovery. **The Twelve Steps—A Way Out.** San Diego, CA: Recovery Publications.

Friends in Recovery. **The Twelve Steps for Christians.** San Diego, CA: Recovery Publications.

Kritsberg, Wayne. **The Adult Children of Alcoholics Syndrome.** Deerfield Beach, FL: Health Communications, Inc.

Larson, Earnie and Hegarty, Carol. **Days of Healing—Days of Joy.** New York, NY: Harper/Hazelden.

Lasater, Lane. **Recovery From Compulsive Behavior.** Deerfield Beach, FL: Health Communications, Inc.

Lerner, Rokelle. **Daily Affirmations—For Adult Children of Alcoholics.** Deerfield Beach, FL: Health Communications, Inc.

Pollard, Dr. John K., III. **Self Parenting: Your Complete Guide to Inner Conversations.** Malibu, CA: Generic Human Studies Publishing.

Smith, Ann W. **Grandchildren of Alcoholics—Another Generation of Codependency.** Deerfield Beach, FL: Health Communications, Inc.

Wegscheider-Cruse, Sharon. **Learning To Love Yourself.** Deerfield Beach, FL: Health Communications, Inc.

Whitfield, Charles. **Healing the Child Within.** Deerfield Beach, FL: Health Communications, Inc.

Woititz, Janet. **Adult Children of Alcoholics.** Deerfield Beach, FL: Health Communications, Inc.

Woititz, Janet G. **Struggle For Intimacy.** Deerfield Beach, FL: Health Communications, Inc.

ORDER FORM

CODE	TITLE	QTY	UNIT PRICE	TOTAL
4001	The Big Book, Alcoholics Anonymous	_____	$ 6.00	_____
4002	Twelve Steps—Twelve Traditions	_____	$ 5.00	_____
1016	Codependent No More	_____	$ 9.95	_____
1058	It Will Never Happen To Me	_____	$ 3.95	_____
2091	Bradshaw on: The Family	_____	$ 9.95	_____
2228	Leaving The Enchanted Forest: The Path From Relationship Addiction To Intimacy	_____	$10.95	_____
4097	The Journey Within—A Spiritual Path To Recovery	_____	$ 8.95	_____
1085	Adult Children—The Secrets of Dysfunctional Families	_____	$ 8.95	_____
9901	The 12 Steps—A Way Out	_____	$14.95	_____
9902	The 12 Steps for Adult Children	_____	$ 7.95	_____
9903	The Twelve Steps—A Spiritual Journey	_____	$14.95	_____
9904	The Twelve Steps for Christians	_____	$ 7.95	_____
1038	The ACoA Syndrome	_____	$ 3.95	_____
3087	Days of Healing—Days of Joy	_____	$ 7.95	_____
2111	Recovery From Compulsive Behavior	_____	$ 7.95	_____
3024	Daily Affirmations—For Adult Children of Alcoholics	_____	$ 6.95	_____
6083	Self Parenting: Your Complete Guide to Inner Conversations	_____	$ 9.95	_____
2026	Grandchildren of Alcoholics/Another Generation of Codependency	_____	$ 8.95	_____
1027	Learning To Love Yourself	_____	$ 7.95	_____
1029	Healing the Child Within	_____	$ 8.95	_____
1034	Adult Children of Alcoholics	_____	$ 6.95	_____
1075	Struggle For Intimacy	_____	$ 6.95	_____

Sub-Total _____

*Sales Tax _____

**Shipping & Handling _____

TOTAL _____

Send this order form and a check or money order for the total to:

TOOLS FOR RECOVERY
1201 Knoxville Street
San Diego, CA 92110

To order by phone, please call
(800) 873-8384 or (619) 275-1350

Name: _____

Address: _____

City/State: _____

Zip: _____ Phone: (_____) _____

*6% Sales Tax (CA Residents only)
**Shpg. & Hand. Min. Charge — $3.00
    Orders over $25.00 — $5.00
    Orders over $50.00 —   6% of Total

Visa and MasterCard Accepted

Bankcard # _____

Expiration Date _____

Signature _____

Allow 2-3 weeks for delivery — UPS